Toward A Christian View Of A Scientific World

Fifteen Topics For Study

George L. Murphy

CSS Publishing Company, Inc., Lima, Ohio

TOWARD A CHRISTIAN VIEW OF A SCIENTIFIC WORLD

Scripture quotations unless marked otherwise are from the *New Revised Standard Version of the Bible*, copyright 1989 by the Division of Christian Education of the National Council of the Churches of Christ in the USA. Used by permission.

Scripture quotations marked TEV are from the *Good News Bible*, in Today's English Version. Copyright © American Bible Society 1966, 1971, 1976. Used by permission.

Scripture quotations marked RSV are from the *Revised Standard Version of the Bible*, copyrighted 1946, 1952 ©, 1971, 1973, by the Division of Christian Education of the National Council of the Churches of Christ in the USA. Used by permission.

Library of Congress Cataloging-in-Publication Data

Murphy, George L., 1942-
  Toward a Christian view of a scientific world : fifteen topics for study / George L. Murphy.
     p.   cm.
  Includes bibliographical references.
  ISBN 0-7880-1807-8 (alk. paper)
  1. Religion and science. 2. Christianity—Philosophy. I. Title
BL240.2 .M844 2001
261.5'5—dc21   00-065115
                                                                          CIP

For more information about CSS Publishing Company resources, visit our website at www.csspub.com.

ISBN 0-7880-1807-8   PRINTED IN U.S.A.

For all who seek
to understand the world
in the light of Christ

Table Of Contents

Preface

"Religion and science" has become a very popular topic in recent years, with books, journals, conferences, and college courses dealing with the topic from different points of view. A great deal of this discussion has been carried on by academic theologians and scientists, and there are not a lot of suitable resources which will enable Christians who aren't experts in one discipline or another to get into it. I believe that it is very important for members of the church to be informed about ways in which Christian faith can address the issues to which modern science and technology give rise, so that the church can carry out its mission in a scientific world. This book is written to provide an introduction to the dialogue between Christian faith and natural science which can be used either by classes in congregations or for individual study.

Some of the topics dealt with here are ones which most people would expect in such a book, including the big bang theory, biological evolution, genetic engineering, and the environment. I have given some background for these topics with discussions of the different ways in which science and theology claim to know their subjects, a proposal about what it means to say that God acts in the world, and some comments on reading the Bible. I have also provided two chapters, numbers 12 and 13, on more speculative topics which are outside the main current of discussion but which should be of interest to some readers.

There has been no attempt to provide detailed references for all the ideas discussed here: the few endnotes are to give the sources of some quotations and to provide clarification on some points. Unless otherwise noted, the New Revised Standard Version of the Bible is used. At the end I have listed some books for further reading, with brief explanatory comments, for those who would like to get into the science-theology dialogue in greater detail and look at some different approaches.

An introductory discussion of topics which are often controversial needs to be developed in interaction with interested learners. I am grateful to members of St. Mark Lutheran Church in Tallmadge, Ohio, and St. Paul's Episcopal Church in Akron, Ohio, as well as to students at Trinity Lutheran Seminary and The Lutheran Theological Seminary at Philadelphia, and colleagues in the ministry, who have attended classes and workshops which I have led. Their questions, suggestions, and encouragement have been very helpful in the development of this book.

Chapter 1

What Are The Questions?

A few years ago, data gathered by satellite-borne instruments gave strong support to the big bang theory about the early universe. "We've seen the face of God," said the astrophysicist in charge of the project when he announced the discovery.

More recently, the cloning of an adult sheep was announced by Scottish scientists. Talk shows and newspapers responded by inviting opinion makers to address the question, "Should we play God?"

Prominent biologists publish popular books about the theory of evolution. Some of them claim that this theory has eliminated any need for us to believe in creation. The claim is that since evolution is a random process, there is no way that a purposeful God could have been involved in the development of life.

Concerns about the environment continue to stir debate. Some people insist that there can't be any huge environmental disaster because God is in control of things. Others argue that religious ideas are partly responsible for our problems of pollution and destruction of nature.

All of these reports have one thing in common: a connection between scientific discoveries and religious beliefs. People have different ideas about whether science is good or bad, and the same is true for religion. But there is a very general sense that there is some connection between scientific discoveries about the world and what is most basic and most important in life. Many articles in popular magazines have spoken about the relationships between religion and science. The cover story of *Newsweek*'s July 20, 1998, issue, for example, was "Science Finds God."

Though we began with some items of recent news, the relationship between science and religion goes far back in history. Unfortunately that relationship has too often seemed to be that of the title of an influential book written by Andrew Dickson White at the end of the nineteenth century: *A History of the Warfare of Science with Theology in Christendom*. Just a mention of the names of Galileo or Darwin shows that the "warfare" image has some accuracy. Religious believers have often had difficulty in adjusting to new ideas about the world, and opponents of religion have sometimes been happy to use such developments as weapons.

But there does not have to be a war. Throughout the history of modern science, from the time of Copernicus in the sixteenth century to today, there have been many scientists who have had deep religious faith, and many people of faith who have appreciated the developments which science has made possible. Today positive relationships between science and religion are being explored by many people. It's true that there are some who still think of themselves as warriors, either for God or for atheism, but they are being seen more and more as on the fringes of a growing *dialogue* between science and religion.

The purpose of this book is to serve as an introduction to this dialogue for members of Christian churches. We are not going to be speaking about "religion in general" but about the Christian faith. The relationships between science and other religions, such as Islam or Buddhism, are interesting and important topics, but they are outside the scope of the present discussion.

The fact that this is an *introduction* means that it does not assume any expertise in either science or theology. It does, however, assume some maturity in dealing with issues which can be controversial, and a willingness to discuss challenging questions without being given answers to all of them. At the end of the book there is a brief list of resources which go into science-religion topics in greater detail.

The rather modest goal of the book is indicated by the title. I want to help readers move *toward* a Christian view of science, and make no claim to reach a final understanding of all the matters which are dealt with. It is also significant that the title does not claim to give *the* Christian view of *the* scientific world. There is more than one view of science which can claim to be Christian, and scientists are by no means in complete agreement in their views of the world. I will have accomplished my purpose if those who have read the book feel comfortable hearing about and discussing the types of issues which are introduced here.

The items with which this chapter began give a good idea of some of the important questions in the dialogue between science and religion. What connections may there be between scientific theories of the early universe (perhaps ten to fifteen billion years ago) and belief that God is the creator of all things? Should we use new biological technologies, such as cloning, which science has made possible? Can we understand biological evolution as an aspect of divine creation? How are Christians to understand our place, and the place of our technology, in the natural world? There are questions about how we understand these developments in connection with our faith and questions about what we should do with these developments. We are really involved in a four-way conversation between *science* (our knowledge of the natural world), *technology* (the use of our knowledge to control the forces of nature), *theology* (the way we think about our religious faith), and *ethics* (what we should do).

It's natural for Christians to discuss the issues for their faith which are raised by developments in science and technology. But the conversation goes both ways. If scientists or engineers go beyond the details of their work and start wondering why the laws of nature are as they are, or why anything exists at all, or whether the universe has any meaning, they are asking essentially religious questions. They don't have to ask those questions. A scientist may simply say that the universe is the way we find it, and that asking why there is a universe is a waste of time. But not all scientists are content with that type of limitation.

Scientists, engineers, and health professionals do ask religious questions and sometimes want religious answers. Those answers may come from traditions of eastern religions or New Age thought as well as from Judaism or Christianity. Part of the church's task of witnessing is to be prepared to respond to the questions which people raise, both inside and outside the Christian community.

Before we look at the specific questions sketched here, we need to lay some groundwork for our discussion. First, we'll consider how it is that we can know about things, both about the world and about God. Then we'll take a quick look at the picture of the world which science has given us. After that, we'll talk about how to read the Bible and about ways in which the Christian tradition has understood God to be involved in what goes on in the world. At that point we'll be ready to take on the specific topics we've mentioned and a few others as well. We'll conclude with some thoughts about ways in which all of this may affect the worship, teaching, and life of the church.

Chapters have been kept short, and it should be fairly easy to pick out those dealing with individual topics of interest instead of reading straight through if that suits your purpose. A few questions and discussion starters are given at the end of each chapter. References have been kept to a minimum, and a list of resources follows the final chapter.

Topics For Discussion

1. What do you think are the two or three most important issues which science and technology raise for religious faith?

2. Which is of greater importance: What science enables us to know about the world, or the ways in which science-based technology enable us to control the world?

3. How have churches which you have belonged to dealt with issues raised by science?

Chapter 2

Understanding And Controlling Nature

Human beings have been learning about the world ever since there have been human beings. In that sense, "natural science" is as old as the human race. Knowledge of the motions of sun and moon, of how to make and maintain fire, and of what seeds to plant to get food shows some beginnings of what would eventually be called science. In order to learn these things, we have had to use two of our abilities: the ability to observe the world and the ability to think. We have used our eyes, ears, and other sense organs (with various instruments which expand their range) and our brains. As history has gone on, people have used their senses and their brains to discover new facts about the world and to think out relationships between previously unconnected facts.

People have made a lot of mistakes too. Some things have been accepted as facts for many years, but then have turned out to be wrong. Mice cannot be "spontaneously generated" in a pile of dirty rags and, in spite of appearances, the stars do not all physically move around the earth every 24 hours. Furthermore, the supposed connections which people have made between different facts have sometimes turned out to be faulty. All the labor which today's astrologers put into relating the positions of stars and planets with what happens in people's lives is, we now know, in vain. The world just doesn't work that way.

So understanding of the world has not simply grown ever since the beginnings of the human race. Knowledge has also been lost, sometimes because of lack of interest, sometimes because of social upheavals, and sometimes because certain kinds of knowledge about the world have threatened religious or political beliefs. It is also possible for the authority of some great thinkers to weigh too heavily on later generations. This happened, for example, with the writings of Aristotle in the late Middle Ages. It wasn't the fault of that Greek philosopher of the fourth century B.C. that his scientific ideas came to be so widely accepted that there was a great deal of resistance to any observations or theories which did not agree with them.

What we usually refer to today as "science" had its beginnings in sixteenth century Europe. Scientific thinking did not just start up out of nowhere, but had been developing for a long time. It is, however, convenient to take the work of Copernicus at the middle of that century as the time when science really took off. His idea that the earth went around the sun, rather than the sun around the earth, made possible new developments in astronomy and then in other branches of knowledge.

Scholars have argued about the reasons that science began to grow so rapidly at this time and in this culture. While there were probably many things which contributed to this development, the biblical view of the world and of God's relationship with it was one factor. The idea that the world is basically the good creation of God, though not itself divine, meant that the world was worth studying, and that it would not be sacrilege to do so. This, combined with the mathematics and ideas of rationality inherited from the Greeks, provided the foundations upon which people like Copernicus, Galileo, and Kepler began the construction of modern science. Most of these pioneers of science were deeply committed Christians.

The early scientists had to fight strongly for the principle that real knowledge required careful observation of the world. It was not enough to think about ways the world *might* be, or to produce arguments for the way the world *should* be. We have to pay attention to the way the world *is*. That is crucial for any sort of genuine science.

But we have to do more than just look around us. What if we want to study the way objects fall to the ground, for example? It will be a pretty frustrating task just to go outside and wait for apples to fall off trees or stones to fall from cliffs so that we can observe them. In order to get anywhere, we're going to have to drop things ourselves and watch what happens. Furthermore, we'll have to do this in a systematic way — for example, by dropping a stone from different heights and timing its fall. And we'll have to take some care to keep the wind or anything else from influencing the falling motion. We will have to make *controlled* observations, or *experiments*, in which we concentrate on just one aspect of the world at a time.

One problem with studying falling bodies is that they fall pretty fast. It turns out that an object released from rest near the earth's surface will drop about sixteen feet in the first second. We'll have to have good clocks in order to time this motion. The design of experiments also requires some cleverness. Galileo realized that he could, in effect, slow down the motion of a falling body by having it move down a smooth inclined plane instead of falling straight down. In this way he could measure the times which it took for bodies to move different distances even with the rather crude clocks which were available around the year 1600.

So suppose that we've dropped a lot of objects through different distances and recorded their times of fall. We now have a lot of numbers written in a notebook. What do we do with all these numbers? Do we really understand anything more about falling bodies than we did when we started?

Not necessarily. Scientific knowledge is more than just a collection of data. We also have to think about the information which we've gathered and try to find some pattern in it. The human brain has to come into play with its ability to *reason*, to generalize beyond the observations which have been made and discover their underlying pattern. For Galileo, this led to a mathematical relation between the time during which a body would fall and the distance which it would move during that time. This relation, or law, would not just apply to the experiments which he had made but to other cases of falling bodies which someone else might observe in the future.

As we consider wider and wider ranges of experience, we may find some discrepancies between the relations we've found and new facts. People found that bodies fall at slightly different rates at different points on the earth, dropping slightly more slowly at the tops of mountains than at sea level. These observations force us to change the laws we had previously worked out. A new, and more general, law has to be found.

The procedure that we've sketched here, of controlled observation and thinking about what is observed, is the core of what is usually called "the scientific method." Sometimes this is set out in a highly organized way. First state the problem, then make a hypothesis about it, then collect data and compare the data with the hypothesis. If they disagree, change the hypothesis. If they agree, then the hypothesis is promoted to the status of a "theory." Continuing the same process may get the theory promoted to a "law," while new facts disagreeing with the theory may require us to go back to the beginning and rethink the entire problem.

This sort of description of the scientific method does give a general idea of the ways in which scientists really work, but the scientific method shouldn't be thought of as a recipe or a computer program which must be followed without any deviation. In particular, there is really no rule which tells how the mind must work in order to come up with correct ideas. Some scientists may stick very close to experimental facts, while others may speculate rather freely about possible forms of natural laws, and only later compare their ideas with observation.

Newton knew about Galileo's results on falling bodies but was not content to stop there. He was considering the motion of the moon, and thought (just how he made the connection we can't say for sure) that it would be possible to consider the moon as a body falling *around* the earth, drawn to the earth by the same force which makes an apple fall from a tree to the ground. This was a stroke of genius which extended the idea of gravitation from a force near the earth's surface to something which was effective throughout the universe. But Newton had to delay publishing his discovery for twenty years because some of the data which he had on the size of the earth was wrong, so that the results of his hypothesis at first didn't seem to agree with observations.

Theories can turn out to be wrong: Galileo showed that the old idea that heavy bodies fall faster than light ones was incorrect. And as we have seen in the case of Newton's work, scientific advances can be delayed by errors in observational results. Good scientists will fight for what seems to be an attractive theory or for experimental results which they think have been well tested, but will also be ready to go back to the drawing board if either theories or experiments turn out to be flawed.

It may also be found that a theory is not simply wrong, but is an approximation to a more accurate theory. We know now that Einstein's theory of gravitation is more accurate than Newton's, but Newton's theory is still adequate for discussing the flights of baseballs, the construction of bridges, and for most work in astronomy.

One important aspect of the scientific approach is that, in principle, it can be followed by anyone, anywhere, at any time. While modern science got its start in Europe in the sixteenth and seventeenth centuries, scientific research today is practiced by people all over the world, by men and women of different races and widely varying political and religious beliefs. Our studies of distant galaxies and the past history of the earth give us reason to believe that the same basic laws of nature could have been found by scientists in the galaxy M33 a billion years ago. Even though scientific research may sometimes be kept secret for one reason or another, science itself has a fundamentally *public* character. Scientific knowledge is available to everyone.

The approach to understanding the world which we've described is, in a certain sense, one of taking the world apart. We try to isolate one aspect of the world, such as the fall of a body toward the earth, and work to understand just that particular phenomenon. Sometimes we literally take things apart. In order to understand light, we may break up a beam of white light with a glass prism into the different colors of the spectrum, red through violet. In order to understand how the bodies of plants or animals work, we dissect them and learn about the different parts of the organism.

Some people have been strongly opposed to this procedure. Even if we set aside ethical questions about experimentation on animals, we can ask if we really understand an entire living organism by knowing about its individual parts. After all, when we've taken an animal completely apart, it no longer is the living thing that we wanted to understand. Tolkien's Gandalf tells of how he had challenged another wizard on this point:

"White!" he sneered. "It serves as a beginning. White cloth may be dyed. The white page can be overwritten; and the white light can be broken."

"In which case it is no longer white," said I. "And he that breaks a thing to find out what it is has left the path of wisdom."[1]

The desire for a holistic understanding of the world rather than a fragmented one deserves our attention. The problem is, however, that it's never been possible to make significant progress in understanding the natural world by keeping the whole picture in view from the start. How do we begin to make sense of this fantastically complex system of stones and light and trees and sound and stars and fluids and animals and all the rest? If someone can do this without isolating individual parts of the world and observing them in detail, more power to that philosopher. But so far, that isn't how science has succeeded.

And in many areas it has succeeded! The scientific approach has done far more than simply catalogue a lot of facts about different pieces of nature. It has made it possible for us to develop well-tested theories which encompass considerable chunks of our experience of the world. Perhaps the clearest indication that science can learn genuine truth about reality is the fact that it has been able to predict new phenomena which no one had ever observed before, and have those predictions confirmed by observation. In the nineteenth century the Russian chemist Mendeleev arranged the chemical elements which were known at the time according to their properties in the form of the "periodic table" which is now displayed on the walls of thousands of science classrooms throughout the world. Mendeleev saw that there were gaps in this table which were not filled by any known element, and predicted the existence of these elements and their properties. These predictions were soon confirmed by the discoveries of these new elements.

Science has had a great deal of success with this method of taking the world apart in order to understand how it works. But we should not be content with that. We really do not understand the human brain as a brain if we only know about the individual cells which make it up. It is also important to put things back together, to try to understand the larger subsystems of the world, and eventually all of nature, in its complex totality. That is a more difficult task, and one which science in many areas has just begun.

In the meantime, we should avoid the fallacy of what the British scientist Donald MacKay called "nothing buttery": the claim that living things, or the world, are "nothing but" the pieces into which we have analyzed them. Light is an electromagnetic wave, but the word "starlight" or the religious symbolism of light are not eliminated when we understand how waves travel. Our brains are not "just" three pounds of pinkish-gray tissue, in spite of the fact that tremendous advances have been made in understanding the human mind by studying the physical makeup and functioning of the brain. There is a difference between explaining something and explaining it away.

Our ability to understand how parts of nature function often gives us the ability to *control* nature by the use of technology. The story of technology goes back thousands of years to discoveries such as fire and the wheel, and our remote ancestors were planting grain, using simple machines, smelting metals, and finding medicinal herbs. But before the modern scientific era, developments in technology were generally by trial and error and good luck. Today's inventions are much more likely to result from deliberate research based on scientific knowledge.

The successes of science-based technology are one indication that science actually is telling us something about a real world. Critics who argue that science is just one way of understanding the world, and that other worldviews besides that of modern science are equally valid, may reasonably be asked if those other worldviews have eliminated smallpox or enabled people to walk on the moon. On the other hand, simplistic arguments that "it works" or "we're doing it because we can" don't justify all uses of science-based technology. There is no question that nuclear explosives work. They are the result of great scientific discoveries and brilliant technological development. But science and technology by themselves can't tell us what to do with this discovery.

19

Science makes possible new technologies but the connection between science and technology is not a one way street. Technological developments often lead to new scientific discoveries. At the root of modern science lies not just a philosophical heritage but also the craft tradition. Good clocks, lenses, pumps, and other pieces of equipment made possible many of the discoveries of the early scientists. Today's work in molecular biology or high energy physics would not be possible without very sophisticated experimental apparatus. In general, science and technology must develop together, and it is sometimes hard to discern the boundary between them.

Scientific work today is quite different from that in the time of Galileo. Governments, corporations, and universities fund multimillion dollar research programs in which hundreds of scientists and engineers participate, and modern communications make new discoveries known almost instantly. While the contributions of individuals are vital to this work, fewer and fewer advances are made by solitary thinkers or inventors working in laboratories in their homes. Yet the basic components of scientific work — careful observation and clear thinking — remain the same. And there still may be something mysterious about the way a discovery is made. In the nineteenth century the chemist Kekulé who had been pondering the problem of the structure of the benzene molecule literally *dreamed* the solution, the "benzene ring." But this would not have happened if his conscious mind had not been working hard on the problem. When Kekulé described his discovery, he made it clear that dreams are not a substitute for hard work:

> *Let us learn to dream, gentlemen ... then perhaps we shall find the truth ... but let us beware of publishing our dreams before they have been put to the proof by the waking understanding.*[2]

Topics For Discussion

1. Is it possible to approach scientific questions with a completely open mind? If not, are there any ways in which prejudices can be eliminated or corrected?

2. Discuss the statement by one scientist that the scientific method is doing the best you can with your mind with no holds barred.

3. What is the shape of the earth? What are your reasons for this answer?

4. What technologies are used in worship services in your church? Which of them would not have been in use a hundred years ago?

---

1. J. R. R. Tolkien, "The Fellowship of the Ring" in *The Lord of the Rings*, 2nd ed., (Houghton Mifflin, Boston, 1974), p. 272.

2. Aaron J. Ihde, *The Development of Modern Chemistry* (Harper & Row, New York, 1964), p. 310.

Chapter 3

How Can We
Know About God?

We know about the world from observations of the world and thinking about those observations. To put it in one word, we can say that we know the world from *experience*, if we include in that term our conscious reflection on what happens. As we have seen, this knowledge of the world is, in principle, available to everybody. All human beings can observe the ways in which animals behave, or can drop objects from different heights and measure the time that it takes them to fall certain distances.

How, then, can we know about God?

Some people might object to putting the question in that way. Shouldn't our concern be simply to know God in a personal way, and not to know *about* God as if God were just another academic subject? And it is quite correct that our primary concern should be to have a personal trust in God, not merely to try to understand God. Theology, the attempt to understand what we believe, does not take the place of faith. But there is a proper place for theology. We don't have to understand how God creates in order to believe that God is the creator of the world. But if we want to relate our faith to scientific understandings of the world, we need some understanding of what we believe. Thus we need to think and speak *about* God. So again, how can we know about God?

There are basically two ways to answer that question. The first is to claim that we can know some things about God in essentially the same way that we can learn about things in the world — from our experience, from observation and reason. Many people who have never really thought very much about the question will argue in that way: "Look at how beautiful — or how wonderfully arranged — the world is. Obviously there must have been some intelligent and powerful being who designed and created the whole thing. How could anybody look around at the world and *not* believe in God?"

But of course some people don't believe. There are perceptive and intelligent people, including some great scientists and philosophers, who are either atheists or who are not sure that the world has any creator.

Arguments for the existence of God can be made more formal. We've looked at the way in which scientists have studied falling bodies and ascribe their motion to a gravitational force. Thus gravitation is the cause of the motion of these bodies. But what causes the earth to have this power of gravitational attraction? We may answer that question in terms of some cause, but someone can immediately ask the cause of *that*. Since (the argument goes) there can't be an infinite chain of causes without any *first* cause, there must be a first cause. And that First Cause is what we call "God."

Arguments for God from general human experience have been used for a long time. Paul and Barnabas seem to be speaking in this way to the pagan crowd at Lystra in Acts 14:14-17. These arguments were set out in detail by the great theologian Thomas Aquinas in the thirteenth century. He actually had five such arguments to show that there is a valid *natural knowledge of God* — that is, a knowledge which, like scientific understanding, is in principle available to everyone. Many later Christian thinkers, Roman Catholic and Protestant, have followed a similar course, especially in trying to persuade unbelievers to give a hearing to the Christian message.

Aquinas thought that such arguments could establish the existence of a "First Cause" or an "Unmoved Mover." But he didn't believe that these arguments tell us everything we need to know about God. They say nothing at all about the distinctively Christian belief that God is revealed in the history of Israel and Jesus the Israelite, that God is the Holy Trinity, or that the Son of God died on the cross and was raised from the dead in order for sins to be forgiven. In other words, the natural knowledge of God can take us only so far. It gives us a start, but to know what we really need to know of God, we must have divine *revelation*. We need the sort of revealed knowledge of God which was given to Moses in the burning bush, or which God gave in his self-disclosure in Jesus.

One important difference between such divine revelation and a natural knowledge of God is that revelation is not accessible to everybody in the same way that experience of the world is. Only the people of Israel were present at Mount Sinai when God gave the Law, and only people in first century Palestine could see and hear and touch Jesus of Nazareth. Other people can hear or read witnesses to those events of revelation, but revelation itself is not repeatable in the same way that an experiment on falling bodies is.

So those are the two possible sources of knowledge of God — and of God's will for us, and of the way in which God acts in the world. Which should we depend on? Christians claim to know something about God. Do they have this knowledge from experience, from revelation, or from some combination of the two?

A traditional position has been that which Aquinas took: Our experience of the world can tell us some basic things about God, but revelation is needed if we are to know the true God, the Trinity, who is revealed in Christ. That means that there can be a "natural theology" derived from natural knowledge of God, but that it will play a fairly modest role in the whole of Christian theology.

Many people, especially since the rise of modern science and philosophy, have not been satisfied with such a limited role for a natural knowledge of God. Since science has been so successful in enabling us to understand the world, why shouldn't it be able to go beyond the world to tell us what we need to know of God? The idea that we need revelation given at certain times and places and not at others is offensive to belief in completely general laws of nature. Thus many people have argued for a "natural religion" which is available to everyone, and which is more important than specific details which the Christian, or Muslim, or Hindu traditions may have to add. One of the clearest modern expressions of this idea is that of physicist Paul Davies, who says, "In my opinion science offers a surer path to God than religion."[1]

It is easy to see what the consequences of this move are for Christian faith: Anything distinctively Christian, such as the cross and resurrection of Christ, would become of secondary importance, if not simply irrelevant. Thus this approach, which ultimately dispenses with revelation and requires only a natural knowledge of God, is not really an option for serious Christian faith.

But even those who hold in theory that natural knowledge can be only an introduction to Christian theology frequently allow it to dominate their thinking in critical areas. In the history of Christianity, philosophical ideas — for example, that the divine nature must be perfectly simple and incapable of suffering — have set the agenda for Christian discussion of God. Distinctively Christian beliefs about God — that God is not simply "one" but is a Trinity, and that one of the Trinity "suffered under Pontius Pilate," are then seen as *problems* to be solved rather than fundamental truths which enable us to understand God and God's relationship with the world.

What happens is that when we set out to gain a natural knowledge of God, there is a great temptation to *construct* the type of God which we think God *should* be. And that is precisely the basic human problem which Paul speaks of in Romans 1:18-23:

> *For the wrath of God is revealed from heaven against all ungodliness and wickedness of those who by their wickedness suppress the truth. For what can be known about God is plain to them, because God has shown it to them. Ever since the creation of the world his eternal power and divine nature, invisible though they are, have been understood and seen through the things he has made. So they are without excuse; for though they knew God, they did not honor him as God or give thanks to him, but they became futile in their thinking, and their senseless minds were darkened. Claiming to be wise, they became fools; and they exchanged the glory of the immortal God for images resembling a mortal human being or birds or four-footed animals or reptiles.*

This has often been understood as if Paul were approving or appealing to a natural knowledge of God, but that really misses his point. Paul says that the *evidence* for the true God is there in creation, but that people instead construct their own idols in the form of what they think God should be. They can know that there is a God, but not who that God is. This passage is a judgment upon the problem of human sin, not a description of how we ought to proceed to know God. An attempt to deny that we have this problem falls under precisely the condemnation Paul speaks of.

And when Paul has spoken of this problem, he does not go on to appeal to a correct natural knowledge of God. After discussing human sin in some detail, he immediately goes on in Chapter 3 to talk about the righteousness of God which is revealed in Christ.

Martin Luther had in mind these words of Paul when he set out a distinction between good and bad theology, between the approaches of what he called "theologians of the cross" and "theologians of glory":

> *That person does not deserve to be called a theologian who looks upon the invisible things of God as though they were clearly perceptible in those things which have actually happened. [Rom. 1:20]*
>
> *He deserves to be called a theologian, however, who comprehends the visible and manifest things of God seen through suffering and the cross.*[2]

Luther certainly believed that God is present and active in the good and beautiful things of the world. But he insists that we must first know God in things that seem to us the very *opposite* of the godlike, in "suffering and the cross." That for him is God's fullest revelation. We will explore further the significance of that idea when we encounter things in the natural world which seem to call into question the power and goodness of God.

If natural theology is such a risky enterprise, it might seem best to reject it entirely. That was precisely the course taken by one of the most influential theologians of the twentieth century, Karl Barth. He blamed natural theology for some of the most serious distortions of Christian thought, such as those of the "German Christians" who supported Hitler. There is something to be said for Barth's claim. As we have seen, Paul argues in Romans that the construction of false gods is at the heart of the human predicament.

But a complete rejection of any natural knowledge of God goes too far, because it tends to divorce our understanding of God from any connection with the natural world. Christian thought would be insulated from developments in our scientific understanding. This would avoid any possibility of conflict between theology and science, but at the cost of making Christianity seem irrelevant to the real world.

What is called for is not elimination of natural theology but a firm maintenance of priorities. We know who God is from God's self-revelation in the history of Israel, a history which reaches its high point in the life, death, and resurrection of Jesus of Nazareth. That is what shows us who God is and what God's will for the world is. In the light of that revelation, we may then look at the world as science enables us to understand it, and see there the activity of the God whom we have come to know in Christ. This may help us to understand more fully God's actions and God's purposes. We are not, then, using our understanding of the world to establish faith in God. On the contrary, we *begin* from a standpoint of faith, and then seek to understand more fully the implications of that faith. Instead of starting from a natural knowledge of God and then moving to revelation, we begin from revelation in order to ground further knowledge of God from nature.

In presenting the gospel to those who do not believe in God, Christians may still want to appeal to what happens in the world as evidence for a creator, as Paul and Barnabas did at Lystra. But they should then keep firmly in mind that that is only a preliminary argument, intended to gain a hearing for the prophetic and apostolic witness to Christ. No one should think that it is adequate simply to think that there is a God — as the letter of James (2:19) reminds us.

The nineteenth Psalm can help to remind us of our priorities. It begins with what seems like a clear expression of natural theology:

> *The heavens are telling the glory of God;*
> *and the firmament proclaims his handiwork.*
> *Day to day pours forth speech,*
> *and night to night declares knowledge.*

The first six verses speak about the natural world. But the second half of the psalm sets this in context:

28

The law of the LORD is perfect,
reviving the soul;
the decrees of the LORD are sure,
making wise the simple;

The psalm continues to praise the law as the revelation of God's will in terms which the first part of the psalm does not use for anything learned from observation of nature. Furthermore, while the first half of the psalm speaks simply of "God," the second part uses the covenant name Yahweh, which most translations, following ancient Jewish usage, read as "the LORD." It almost sounds as if the author of the second part of the psalm realized that nature could lead people to think that there is a creator, but wanted to warn against the dangers of thinking that such an understanding of God could stand apart from God's revelation of himself and his will to Israel.

Speaking of God's will reminds us that there is an ethical dimension to all this. To put it simply, God wants us to do some things and not to do other things. Later chapters will deal with decisions that have to be made about the ways to use the technologies which science makes available. How do we make those decisions?

The Bible provides guidance for life's decisions. There is the law given to Israel, which is summed up in the Ten Commandments. The content of the commandments having to do with our relationships with other people is not unique to Judaism or Christianity, for most cultures throughout the world teach that we are not to murder, steal, or commit adultery. This suggests to some people that there is a "natural law" which is given all people. Another source of guidance in the Bible is the wisdom tradition, which is strong in the books of Proverbs and Ecclesiastes, as well as Wisdom and Sirach in the Apocrypha. And again, there are many parallels between this tradition and teachings about wisdom among other cultures of the ancient Near East. Finally, Christians have the example of the life and teachings of Christ in the Gospels.

It is clear though that none of these will give us direct answers to some of the ethical questions which science and technology raise for us. Nuclear energy sources, genetic engineering, and computers simply are not mentioned in the Bible, and we will search there in vain for directions on how to use these technologies.

29

Christians are, however, given the promise of the Holy Spirit. Jesus says that the Spirit "will teach you everything, and remind you of all that I have said to you" (John 14:26). The Spirit will make it possible for the Christian community to connect God's revelation to which Scripture witnesses with the concerns with which the modern world presents us. This does not mean that we can expect ethical answers to be given to us magically. As we will discuss in Chapter 5, God generally works in the world through natural processes. If Christians work together in prayerful and thoughtful ways to discern God's will from Scripture and the insights of Christian teachers of the past, they can trust that the Spirit will be at work in answers which emerge. Chapters 10 and 11 are intended as contributions to this process of deliberation.

Topics For Discussion

1. How does Paul use the idea of a natural knowledge of God in his speech in Athens which is described in Acts 17:16-34?

2. How would you respond to someone who says, "The world is so marvelous that anybody who doesn't believe in a God who made it must be really stupid"?

3. Discuss the following statement by Albert Einstein:

> *Certain it is that a conviction, akin to religious feeling, of the rationality or intelligibility of the world lies behind all scientific work of a higher order. This firm belief, a belief bound up with deep feeling, in a superior mind that reveals itself in the world of experience, represents my conception of God ... Denominational traditions I can only consider historically and psychologically; they have no other significance for me.*[3]

4. What is the significance of the statement that "the fear of the LORD is the beginning of wisdom" (Proverbs 9:10, Psalm 111:10)?

1. Paul Davies, *God And The New Physics* (Simon & Schuster, New York, 1983), p. ix.

2. Martin Luther, "Heidelberg Disputation" in *Luther's Works*, vol. 31 (Philadelphia, Fortress, 1957), p. 40.

3. Albert Einstein, "On Scientific Truth" in *Essays in Science* (Philosophical Library, New York, 1934), p. 11.

Chapter 4

The Scientific Picture Of The World

Before we think about how God acts in the world, we need to consider the description of the world which science gives us today. Nothing like a complete description of modern science can be given here. Furthermore, scientific ideas may change in a few years: A description of the scientific view of the world a century ago would have been quickly outdated by discoveries in physics, astronomy, chemistry, and biology. But we need to sketch the best understanding presently available, so that we can go on to speak of God's action in the real world.

We will try to describe the world in terms of a few basic concepts which most people have some feeling for. There are risks with this procedure, for one of the things science has become aware of is the fact that common-sense ideas are *not* adequate for a description of the world when we get outside the realm of phenomena in which our common sense developed. But we need to begin somewhere and will note non-intuitive ideas as they arise.

Scientific descriptions of the world generally try to describe it in terms of events which take place in *space* and *time*. *Velocity* is the rate at which something moves through space in the course of time. We can describe many of the contents of the world in terms of the concepts of *mass* and *energy*. The mass of a physical system is the amount of matter or substance in that system, without regard to what type of matter it is. (A kilogram of lead and a kilogram of air have the same mass.) Energy is often defined as "the ability to do work" — the ability to change things, to make things happen. A stone has a certain mass. When in motion, it also has a certain amount of energy. We can see this when it collides with another stone and sets it in motion.

The simplest systems are made up of a few bodies like the stones of the previous paragraph. The basic laws which describe how bodies can be arranged in space, and how their positions and velocities can change with time, were given by Newton in the latter half of the seventeenth century. If we know the mass of each body, and where it is and how it is moving at a particular instant, and if we know how the energy of the system depends on the positions and velocities of the bodies, we can calculate how all of the bodies will continue to move in the future.[1] This is how we can find the orbit of a comet, the trajectory of a baseball, or the vibration of a mass connected to a spring.

In Chapter 2 we mentioned another discovery of Newton, the law of gravitational attraction between any two bodies. When this is combined with the laws of motion, the positions of the planets and satellites in the solar system can be calculated for any time in the future. Apparent discrepancies between these calculations and the observed positions of the planet Uranus in the early nineteenth century suggested that there might be another yet unobserved planet whose gravitational attraction was causing these deviations from the theory. This hypothesis was soon confirmed by the telescopic discovery of Neptune.

The great successes of the laws of mechanics led to a sweeping generalization about the world. *If* the positions and velocities of all bodies could be known at a given instant, and if the mathematical expression for the energy were known, the state of the system could be found for all future time. It seemed that the whole future course of the universe was, in principle, laid out and determined. This *determinism* would leave no room for any free choice. Furthermore, it seemed to some that there was nothing for a God to do once the universe had been created: The world machinery would simply go on in accord with the pattern laid down in the laws of motion. There would be no point in praying for rain, because the patterns of atmospheric motion and moisture content would already have been determined when the earth was formed.

We know now that things aren't that simple. The future course of a system can be predicted *if the initial positions and velocities of all bodies are known precisely*. But there are limits to the precision with which we can know those quantities. In some cases this doesn't matter much: a small uncertainty in initial values results only in small errors in predictions of the future. But in other cases, such as the earth's weather system, those predictions are very sensitive to small uncertainties in the initial information. The situation has been described picturesquely in terms of the "butterfly effect": A butterfly flapping its wings in Asia will change the weather in New York a few days later. Since we can never know what all butterflies are doing, we can never have precise and detailed long-range predictions of the weather.

And there are also systems which can't be described adequately in terms of bodies in motion. To describe electric and magnetic phenomena we need the concept of a *field*. While a system like the billiard balls on a table involves only bodies in a few separate parts of space, an *electromagnetic field* is a condition of energy distributed throughout space. This field exists at every point and may change with time. The laws which govern the electromagnetic field were written down in 1865 by James Clerk Maxwell. Besides describing phenomena like static electricity and electromagnetic generators, Maxwell's equations have solutions which represent *electromagnetic waves* travelling through space at a speed of about 300,000 kilometers per second — which is the measured value of the speed of light! Light (like radio signals and X-rays) is an electromagnetic wave which can carry energy from one region of space to another.

Both Newton's mechanics and Maxwell's electromagnetic theory were very successful, but serious problems are encountered if we try to put them together in a comprehensive theory. It seems like common sense, for example, that the speed of light can't be 300,000 km/sec for everyone. If observer A sees a light wave moving at that speed and observer B chases after it at 1,000 km/sec, then B should see the wave travelling at 299,000 km/sec. But this isn't the case. The speed of light in vacuum is found to be the same for all observers, no matter how they're moving. That contradicts our basic common sense ideas of space and time. Albert Einstein realized, at the beginning of the twentieth century, that those common sense ideas of space and time therefore had to be changed.

Common sense is accurate enough for everyday situations, but not when we enter realms of high speeds and intense gravitational fields with which atomic physicists and astronomers deal. Then space and time can no longer be considered as separate and absolute, but are interconnected. Einstein's *relativity theory* predicts, for example, that an observer will see a moving clock run more slowly than a stationary one. While this is contrary to our intuition, it has now been confirmed by observations of radioactive decays of rapidly moving particles.

Einstein took a further step away from common-sense ideas of space and time when he explained gravitation in terms of *space-time curvature*. The presence of matter affects measurements of space and time, so that the geometry of Euclid is not valid. (For example, the sum of the angles of a triangle is not 180°.) In the vicinity of the earth, Einstein's theory predicts only tiny deviations from our everyday ideas of geometry or Newton's theory of gravitation. In extreme situations like collapsed stars or the early stages of the universe, however, the newer theory has important implications, as we will see in a later chapter.

One of the most important aspects of Einstein's theory is summed up in his famous equation $E = mc^2$. Mass m is related to energy E via the speed of light c. The basic concepts of "amount of matter" and "ability to change the state of matter" are identified. This has profound implications for our understanding of what matter *is*, especially when combined with other insights into the atomic and sub-atomic worlds.

Chemists gained a great deal of information about the nature of matter with the hypothesis that substances are made up of atoms, a different type for each chemical element. This made it possible to understand many basic properties of chemical reactions between different substances in terms of the ways in which atoms might combine to form molecules. We have already seen how Mendeleev's periodic table revealed some of the patterns of chemical properties of the elements, and thus pointed to some not-yet-discovered patterns of atomic structure.

A great deal of progress could be made just by considering atoms to be hard little balls, without worrying about how atoms themselves might be constructed. The original idea of atoms proposed by some ancient Greek philosophers was that they were indivisible — the Greek *atomos* means "uncuttable." But evidence that atoms did have some internal structure, that they were composed of smaller electrically charged particles, revealed a profound problem: According to Newton's mechanics and Maxwell's electromagnetic theory, it is impossible for atoms to exist! An atom constructed in accord with these theories would collapse in a tiny fraction of a second.

We've all seen the familiar "picture" of an atom with electrons circling a nucleus like the planets going around the sun. This is an early atomic model developed by Neils Bohr, in which he made use of an idea introduced earlier to solve some problems about the nature of light. Planck and Einstein had suggested that light behaved as if it were made up of particles, called *quanta* or photons, whose energy was related to the color of the light. This was an early form of *quantum theory*.

The fully-developed form of this theory involves radical departures from common-sense understanding of the world, and even from ideas of what it *means* to understand the world. We just noted, for example, that light sometimes behaves as if it is made up of particles. But we saw earlier that light sometimes behaves as a wave spread out through space. Somehow it seems capable of either type of behavior, though never both at the same time. And this duality does not just apply to light. Things usually described as "particles," such as electrons and protons, also have a wavelike character. What is "waving" in these waves is *probability* — the chances of finding a particle at various points. Instead of picturing an atom as electrons orbiting a nucleus, we have to think of a small cloud of probability oscillating around the nucleus.

This might make quantum theory sound vague and imprecise. Nothing could be farther from the truth. Even though the theory gives up the attempt to state precisely where a particle is and how fast it is moving, its equations are able to make extremely accurate predictions about the light emitted from atoms and the ways in which atoms can bind together in chemical reactions. Quantum theory has been tremendously successful in explaining the properties of matter and light and their interactions.

The study of radioactivity, pioneered by Marie Curie and other scientists around 1900, enabled them to penetrate even more deeply, into the nucleus of the atom. An understanding of phenomena on this scale requires both relativity and quantum theory. Matter is made up of interactions, and these interactions are described in terms of probabilities. Physicists have been able to develop a fairly comprehensive model in which there are three basic interactions: gravitation, described by Einstein's theory — though further work is needed to make this compatible with quantum theory; electroweak, a combination of Maxwell's electromagnetism and the "weak" force responsible for some radioactive decays; and the strong interaction, which holds the atomic nucleus together. There are also two basic types of matter: quarks, which combine to form protons, neutrons, and more exotic particles, and leptons, of which the electron is the most important.

It was realized in the nineteenth century that heat could be understood as the mechanical energy of microscopic atoms and molecules. The *first law of thermodynamics*, the law of conservation of energy, says that the total amount of energy in a closed system (that is, a physical system which receives or gives nothing to its surroundings) will always remain the same. In particular, the total energy of the universe will not change. Heat may be converted to mechanical work, as in a steam engine, but energy cannot be created or destroyed. The *second law of thermodynamics*, however, says that the total amount of *useful* work in a closed system can never increase, and in general will decrease. In the operation of any steam or internal combustion engine, for example, some energy is always wasted in the exhaust. We will see some important implications of these laws later.

To this point we have been describing the physical world as it is in our immediate neighborhood of space and at the present time. But we can try to extend this understanding outward in space and back in time to see if we can make sense of larger regions. As geologists dig into the earth, they find that the rocks occur in layers, or *strata*, of different types. It would take a long time for these strata to be formed by natural processes, such as the slow deposition of silts at the bottom of oceans. It is very suggestive that different layers of rock contain different *fossils*, the remains of plants and animals which no longer live on earth. The dinosaurs, of course, are the most famous of these. This suggests that the earth has been in existence for a very long time, and that different plant and animal species have developed and then become extinct over many generations, to be replaced by new species.

The earth's age can be estimated from the abundances of radioactive elements. Since the rates of decay of these elements are known, we can estimate how long it has taken for their abundances to reach their present values. For example, only one uranium atom out of 140 is the lighter U-235, while the rest are U-238. This is because U-235 decays much more rapidly than U-238.[2] From the abundances and lifetimes of the two types of uranium we can conclude that the material of the solar system was formed around six billion (6,000,000,000) years ago. The age of the earth is about four and a half billion years.

Fossils and radioactive elements are "time capsules" which give us information about our planet's history. When we turn our view from earth to outer space, we find that we are looking into the past in a quite literal sense because it takes light time to get to us. We see the bright star Sirius as it was about nine years ago. If a *light year* is defined as the distance which light travels in a year, Sirius is about nine light years away. Our Milky Way galaxy contains about a hundred billion stars, spread out over a region about 100,000 light years across.

And this is only one of billions of galaxies, spread out in all directions to distances of at least ten billion light years. This means that the light which we receive from the farthest objects we can detect has been in transit since before the earth was formed.

The universe is very big and very old. But it is also changing. On the earth, the plates carrying the continents drift slowly on the lower plastic layers of the planet. Systematic shifts in the light which we detect from more and more distant galaxies indicate that they are all receding from one another, as if from a gigantic explosion. This *big bang*, which seems to mark the beginning of our physical universe, took place between ten and fifteen billion years ago. The significance of this fact for religious understandings of creation will be discussed in a later chapter.

I have given here a very sketchy look at the picture of the physical world which scientists have built up — with one important exception. Except for a reference to fossils, nothing has been said about *life*. The contributions of the biological sciences to our picture of the world have been omitted.

We might begin to remedy that omission with a definition of "life," but we would soon find ourselves bogged down. It isn't easy to give a precise definition which includes all those things and only those things that we want to call "alive." This isn't as much of a problem as one might think, for understanding things doesn't depend on what we *call* them. In fact, we follow the old rule, "If it walks like a duck and quacks like a duck, it's a duck." There are borderline phenomena about which there is some debate, such as viruses. Sometimes these act alive, as when they're multiplying inside a cell. But at other times they are inertly arranged in crystalline form. Scientists simply try to understand how viruses are constructed and what they do, and how they may be related to other systems. Philosophers can argue about whether or not they're alive.

We can, however, note several important features of living things. They are physical systems composed of matter (for we are not considering angels now), and all of them that we know of make use of the element carbon in essential ways, as well as hydrogen, oxygen, nitrogen, and other elements. Living things are made of the same types of atoms as non-living ones. They are alive not because they are made of any special "vital" material but because of the arrangement and functioning of the material.

Living things are complex structures through which there are flows of mass and energy. They take in substances and energy (perhaps in the form of energy locked up in chemical compounds) which they need and excrete waste material and energy. Living things are not static and are not in equilibrium with their environment. ("To assume room temperature" is sometimes used as a euphemism for "to die.")

40

Living things also have the ability to grow and reproduce. So do crystals — but there is a big difference. Crystals grow simply by having more atoms or molecules of the same type added to them. Living things carry *information* which enables their molecular machinery to construct new systems of the same types from basic chemicals. This information can be modified as well, so that offspring need not be exactly like parents — a critical fact for any understanding of changes in living things over the generations.

Much of the work of earlier biologists was the study of plants and animals as a whole. This enabled them to discern relations between the hundreds of thousands of species which presently exist on earth, as well as the numerous species which have become extinct. But many of the advances made during the twentieth century have involved studies of life at the molecular level. At this level many of the processes are the same regardless of the species which is being considered or even whether it is a plant or an animal: The distinction between botany and zoology is not fundamental for molecular biology.

Two types of molecules in particular are important for life. *Proteins* are complex molecules composed of units called *amino acids*, of which there are about twenty types. A protein is made by stringing these amino acids together in a certain order. These long strings of molecules are often folded in complicated ways, and their shapes play important roles in their functions. Proteins serve both as structural materials (for example, in muscle fiber) and as the crucial enzymes which enable the chemical reactions necessary for life to be carried out. Especially important are the reactions by which cells are able to make use of the chemical energy in their nutrients, converting this energy to forms which can run the cellular machinery.

The second type of molecule is the *nucleic acids*, which carry the information needed to construct proteins. Each of our cells contains deoxyribonucleic acid or *DNA*, the famous "double helix" molecule. Each strand of this long molecule has encoded, in the pattern of molecular units from which it is built up, the information which enables the machinery to construct the proteins which the cell needs to function.

In the 1860s the Moravian monk Gregor Mendel was able to work out some of the basic laws of *genetics* by experiments on the breeding of pea plants. He suggested that organisms contain *genes* which they contribute to their offspring, and which determine physical properties such as flower color, shape of seed, and so forth. We can now identify these genes with portions of the DNA molecule. In human beings they do not code for complex traits like musical ability, but for the construction of particular proteins. Eye color, for example, is hereditary because there are genes which control the production of a certain pigment. It is the total effect of all the genes which parents contribute to offspring which determines the hereditary endowment of that offspring. Debates about the extent to which the offspring is determined by "nature" in this way and how much is due to "nurture" still continue.

The genetic revolution which is continually breaking into the daily news is not, however, just a matter of new understandings of hereditary processes. Geneticists are able to manipulate and combine DNA in order to influence what will be produced. This work in *genetic engineering* ranges from artificial production of important proteins such as human growth hormone and insulin to the hotly debated possibility of human cloning. We will discuss some of the theological and ethical dimensions of this work in a later chapter.

We have concentrated here on basic properties of life at the molecular and cellular level, but the complexity of living things is seen in the ways in which cells are combined to form tissues and organs, and the ways in which these go together to make whole living organisms, such as oak trees and elephants. And in an important sense the process does not stop there. The discipline of ecology studies the ways in which different organisms, and different types of organisms, interact. Ecologists study not just individual plants and animals but *ecosystems*, composed of plants and animals which eat the plants and predators who eat those animals and other plants which get nutrients from the decay of organisms in the system. Such a system is not static but changes in somewhat predictable ways, as in the sequence of plants which will grow in an area after a forest fire. Some people have gone beyond this to talk about the entire earth as a living thing, but that is rather speculative at present.

As in our description of the physical world, we have concentrated first on the basic phenomena of life as they are today. Those basic processes of heredity and metabolism have remained pretty much the same for millions of years, but the types of organisms in which they have been expressed have not. As we have already seen, geological strata show us that the plants and animals which lived millions of years in the past were different from those alive today. The first traces of living things can be dated to about three and a half billion years in the past, about a billion years after the earth was formed. For most of the history of life on earth there were only single-celled organisms, but multicellular life came on the scene around a billion years ago, resulting in a relatively rapid proliferation of complex organisms.

All of this suggests that there has been some sort of *biological evolution* going on — that offspring differ from the parent generation in ways that accumulate over time, until new species come into being. Such ideas had been around for centuries, but the modern theory of evolution started in 1858 when Charles Darwin and Alfred William Wallace separately proposed the idea of evolution through *natural selection*. This means that there is variation among members of a species, and environmental conditions serve as a type of "filter" to determine which are more likely to survive and to have offspring to which they pass on their characteristics. This theory has been widely accepted by biologists as providing a generally accurate picture of the way in which life has developed on earth, and of the relationships between different species.

There has been a great deal of religious controversy about evolutionary theories, and we will consider some of the issues in a later chapter. But now, having given a very short sketch of the world, we need to talk about ways of understanding divine activity in that world.

Topics For Discussion

1. We're usually suspicious of the ideas of a person who "has no common sense." The basic ideas of relativity and quantum theory seem contrary to common sense. When is "common sense" a good guide and when isn't it?

2. Galileo found that a body will continue to move in a straight line at constant speed *unless* a force acts on it. Before then people thought that a force was needed to *keep* a body in motion. Why do you suppose they thought that? Which idea seems to be more in accord with everyday experience?

3. One argument sometimes made against evolution is, "If apes evolved into humans, why are there still any apes?" Comment on this.

4. Is it likely that scientists will ever get to a correct "theory of everything" which explains all phenomena in the universe?

---

1. This is the form in which the equations of motion were expressed by William Rowan Hamilton in the nineteenth century rather than that originally given by Newton.

2. These are two of the *isotopes* of uranium, one whose nucleus has a mass of 235 atomic mass units and the other 238. The former is the type from which nuclear weapons can be made. The *half-life* of U-235, the time within which half the atoms in a given sample will decay, is about 700,000,000 years, while that of U-238 is over six times as long, 4,500,000,000 years.

Chapter 5

God's Action In The World

Christians say in the Apostles' Creed, "I believe in God, the Father almighty, creator of heaven and earth." This immediately introduces the issue of *creation*, which has been at the center of science-religion debates for many years. When we hear the word "creation" we are likely to think back to events of the distant past and begin to ask whether theories of a big bang or evolution can be reconciled with Genesis. But let us move more slowly.

What does it mean to say that we believe in God as creator? In his *Small Catechism*, Martin Luther gave a very down-to-earth answer:

> *I believe that God has created me together with all creatures. God has given me and still preserves my body and soul: eyes, ears, and all limbs and senses; reason and all mental faculties. In addition, God daily and abundantly provides shoes and clothing, food and drink, house and home, spouse and children, fields, livestock, and all property — along with all the necessities and nourishment for this body and life. God protects me against all danger and shields and preserves me from all evil. God does all this out of pure, fatherly, and divine goodness and mercy, without any merit or worthiness of mine at all! For all of this I owe it to God to thank and praise, serve and obey him. This is most certainly true.*[1]

"All creatures" must include extinct animals and distant galaxies, but those are not the things Luther concentrates on. Creation means for me, first of all, that God provides for me the things which I need for life. In other words, the Catechism emphasizes not the origin of things but *providence*, God's provision for creatures. We will go on to questions of origins, but this is where we begin.

A little reflection will show that the course which our theological reflection takes here is similar to that taken by science. Modern science did not begin by trying to solve the problem of the beginning of the universe or the origin of life. Instead, scientists studied phenomena in their own neighborhood of space and time, observing falling bodies, combining chemicals, and classifying plant specimens. Only gradually did their understanding stretch out into space and back into the past. Science succeeded by understanding first what went on in our space-time vicinity, and then trying to extend that understanding further. It is worth seeing if a similar procedure can be helpful theologically.

So what do we mean when we say, for example, that God gives us food? God's people have always believed that God *does* do this, a faith which the Jewish table prayer expresses: "Blessed art thou, O LORD our God, King of the universe, who bringest forth bread from the earth." But they have also always known that they usually will not have bread if seeds are not planted, if there is no rain, or if the work of harvesting is not done. Somehow God's provision for us has some connection with the regular processes of nature and the work which people do.

Today we understand in considerable detail the complex network of processes which end up with bread on our table. Nuclear reactions in the core of the sun release energy which eventually comes to the earth in sunlight and is used by plants in photosynthesis to produce organic molecules from water and carbon dioxide. DNA in each cell of the plant contains the information which enables the cellular machinery to operate, for cells to divide, and the plant to grow. The laws of mechanics and thermodynamics describe the atmospheric patterns which help to determine whether the plant will live or die. The human work of farming, milling, baking, and marketing eventually gets the bread into the shopping cart.

Where is God in all that? There is no single link of that network called "God" which must be excluded from the study of genetics or weather or economics. And it will not work simply to say that God got everything going in the beginning: Such an idea would be quite inadequate to express the belief that God is active in the world today, so that it means something to address God as the one who "brings forth bread from the earth." If we are to be able to say this, we must somehow understand God to be at work in, with, and under the natural processes which science studies.

One traditional way of speaking about this is to say that God works through natural processes as instruments. Just as a carpenter works with a hammer and saw, God works with the things in the world to carry out God's purposes. Both the carpenter and the saw are actually at work, though in different ways, to bring about whatever is done.

That is a very simple picture, and some qualifications must be made. First, there is a crucial difference between a human being working with a tool and God working with natural processes: Belief that God is the creator means that everything ultimately depends for its existence on God. In the last analysis, God is the maker of every tool God uses. (Don't be surprised if it is hard to see any parallel between this and the activity of a human worker. That is just the point — while there are some parallels between human and divine action, there are also fundamental differences.)

We don't want to picture this simply as a two-stage process in which God first makes instruments exist and then works with them. We saw in our brief sketch of science that the world is fundamentally dynamic, not static. The structures at the most basic level involve real and potential interactions. For example, a "bare electron," completely isolated from anything else, is a theoretical fiction. A real electron is a result of interactions of that unobservable "bare" particle with the electromagnetic field and other particles. Thus it is better to try to picture God as keeping things in existence precisely by working with them.

The "tools" which God uses at the most fundamental level are not things like hammers and saws which obey Newton's laws of mechanics. At the atomic level, God's tools obey the laws of quantum mechanics with their inherent fuzziness, and even at the level of everyday occurrences they display phenomena like the butterfly effect. Since there is not rigid determinism built into the world's machinery, God has some freedom to act even without going outside the bounds of what the laws of nature allow.

But it seems that God does, in the vast majority of cases, restrict the divine action to what can be accomplished by natural processes. We could imagine God doing all kinds of unpredictable things in random ways with the materials of the world. Things might fall up and frogs might speak English. But such things happen — to put it cautiously — very seldom, if at all.

This suggests that God *limits* himself to act within the bounds of rational laws, laws which themselves have God as their source. This does not mean that God could not by nature do other than that, but that God *chooses* to limit the divine action. As we have seen, this still leaves God some flexibility, but there are some things which will not happen.

But why would God so limit his activity? Think of the consequences if this were not the case — if God acted in arbitrary and unpredictable ways. Such a world would be a nightmare. We would never have any idea what to expect of it. We wouldn't know when the sun would rise or which foods were nutritious and which poisonous. God might always act to shield us from any harm and from any consequences of our actions, but then we would be like babies in a nursery, continually presented with things from who knows where. We would never be able to reach any kind of maturity in the world. And in particular, science would be impossible.

Thus this divine self-limitation is a tremendous gift of God. It is *grace*. Because of it we are able to understand our world on its own terms. It is possible for us to live as adult citizens of the world, and not as children or pets.

That means also that it is possible for us to ignore God, or refuse even to acknowledge God's existence, and still understand the world. The God who works in this way is a God who does not force creatures to recognize the existence of the creator. God takes the chance of being ignored. That is the price which God pays for the gift of understanding which we receive.

This is an expression of the same fundamental theme which we encounter when we discuss redemption, the self-giving and self-sacrificing character of God. "For the Son of Man also came not to be served but to serve, and to give his life a ransom for many" (Mark 10:45). This should not be surprising if we remember that all God does in the world is a work of the whole Trinity, Father, Son, and Spirit. Thus God's everyday activity in the world bears the mark of the One who "emptied himself" of divine prerogatives and was willing to be seen as one who had merely "the form of a slave" (Philippians 2:7). It is the mark of the cross.

And just as it is only faith which sees God's saving power in the cross (1 Corinthians 1:23-24), it is faith which sees God at work in the natural processes of the world. Scientific observation sees those processes and scientific reasoning is able to understand them in detail, but science cannot see the God who works with and through those processes. That is why we say in the creeds that we "believe" — not that we "understand" — God to be the creator.

Thus there are three aspects to God's activity in nature. God works through natural processes as instruments and generally limits his activity to what can be accomplished through those processes, so that we see God at work in the world only through faith. It is important to keep all three aspects in mind, for otherwise we may go to the extremes either of thinking that God's work in the world is something which we can prove scientifically, or that God isn't doing anything at all in the world.

This type of theological explanation is adequate as far as it goes. However, it raises a couple of difficult issues which may have already occurred to the reader.

One of the oldest problems of humanity, which goes back at least to the Book of Job, is "Why do bad things happen to good people?" More generally, why is there so much evil in the world if God is good? If God really is active in everything that happens, as we have said, why doesn't everything work out well? The most pointed way of posing the question is to ask how a good God can work with natural processes which bring about evil consequences.

It is always a bit presumptuous to try "to justify ways of God to men," as Milton thought he could do in *Paradise Lost*. But there are a couple of suggestions we can make here. First, the presence of evil in the world is a price we pay for living in a world which we can understand. It might seem that it would be wonderful to live in a world in which we were always protected from cancer and tornadoes and other natural disasters, but that could come about only if

God refused to let the natural processes of the world have any integrity. What would the world be like if God worked with the chemical reactions which make fire burn in order for us to cook our food, but stopped them from burning a house? As we have already seen, such a world would appear chaotic and incomprehensible to us. We would be kept in an infantile state.

Similar considerations apply to *moral* evils, caused by human choice, as to *natural* evils like bad weather and disease. If God stopped allowing our brains and bodies to function in order to keep us from doing anything bad, we would simply not be human beings. Not only would we be unable to understand the world, we would be unable even to understand ourselves.

I have spoken of the price which we pay in order to live in a lawful and understandable world. But that is not by any means the greatest price. In the Christian story, *God* pays that price by coming into the world to participate in human life in Jesus of Nazareth. God does not simply stand outside the world, but enters it and is at the receiving end of evil. The focus of each of the Gospels is the Passion story, in which the Son of God suffers and dies a painful death. We will have more to say about this when we discuss evolution and the place of human life in the universe.

This all perhaps makes some sense of the fact that God is good yet does not continually work miracles in order to avert evil. But that raises just the opposite question: The Bible and the later Christian tradition (as well as traditions of other religions) are full of accounts of miraculous events. Can we explain this in any way which is connected with our discussion of the divine activity in the world? Or do we just have to throw our hands up and say, "It's a miracle"?

This is not the place for a detailed treatment of miracles, which would require careful study of the relevant texts in the Old and New Testaments. For each miracle story we would need to give attention to the nature of the account and try to decide whether or not it was to be understood as historical. All we can do here is to see how we might think of miraculous events taking place.

There is really a range of possibilities for understanding miracles. At one end of the spectrum is the attempt to explain the miracle purely in terms of known physical processes. This is plausible in some cases. The great event of the passage of the Sea of Reeds in the Exodus, for example, is made possible because "The LORD drove the sea back by a strong east wind all night, and turned the sea into dry land; and the waters were divided" (Exodus 14:21). At least the basic physical phenomenon here could be understood as a natural meteorological event happening at just the right time. At the other end of the spectrum, miracles are sometimes spoken of simply as "violations of the laws of nature" — i.e., things which are quite beyond the possibilities of natural processes. The resurrection of Jesus might seem to be the clearest example of this.

But there is a middle ground. It is possible that some events which we judge as miraculous are very rare but "natural" occurrences whose possibility God has built into the laws of nature. This would be consistent with the fact that many miracles are in fact "the same type of thing" which takes place all the time, but in a greatly magnified or speeded up way. Jesus' feeding of the 5,000 in the Gospels is like what happens every year when a little grain is planted as seed and gives rise to a much greater amount of grain. But in this case, it takes place without all the intermediate steps. And it is this resemblance which shows that the one who performs the miracle is to be identified with the one who makes the grain grow in the fields all the time. He is not "intervening" in creation as some sort of foreign intruder, but through his actions reveals himself as the world's creator.

This chapter has concentrated on possible ways of understanding God's action in the world today. No attention has been given to the beginning of life or the formation of the earth. We are going to go on to apply the ideas of this chapter to what the Bible and science have to say about origins — the origin of the universe, of life, and of humanity. But first we'll take a quick look at some things to keep in mind as we read the Bible.

Topics For Discussion

1. In an old collection of teachings of Jewish rabbis there is the statement that one of the things God made at the end of the sixth day of creation was "the tongs made with tongs." Does this rather mysterious phrase help in picturing the way God works through natural processes which God has created?

2. There are other ways of thinking about divine action besides those described in this chapter. We might say that religion and science are two different languages for describing what happens in the world. In one language we talk about natural processes, and in the other about God doing things. Discuss this idea.

3. If weather is a result of natural processes which are described by the laws of physics, does it make any sense to pray for rain?

----

1. *A Contemporary Translation of Luther's Small Catechism* (AugsburgFortress, Minneapolis, 1996), p. 21.

Chapter 6

Reading The Bible

We are going to move now from the general topic of God's action in the world to issues of origins — the development of the physical universe and biological evolution. In a very important sense our discussions of these issues will be applications of what we have said about God's work in the world today. If God acts through natural processes now, it is reasonable to consider the possibility that God was working in that way in the distant past as well. We will find that that idea actually works quite well.

However, we should not move too quickly. The ultimate source for Christian doctrine is to be Scripture, and we will therefore need to consider seriously what the Bible says about the origins of the universe and of life. There are some pitfalls in doing that, and perhaps even more danger of unconsciously moving along well-trodden but misdirected paths. In order to avoid those dangers, we should do a little thinking about the ways in which we read the Bible.

We do need to take the Bible with utmost seriousness. Scripture is true and authoritative, and it is not a live option for Christians simply to ignore or discard parts of it which for one reason or another they find inconvenient. But to say that the Bible is truthful does not answer all the questions we have when we read it.

We should first realize the diversity of types of literature found in the Bible. Failure to do this is behind much of the misunderstanding and conflict in the science-religion area. Many people assume without thinking about it that the only way for a biblical text to be *true* is for it to be an accurate historical account of events which have actually taken place. It must, as they often say, "be taken literally" in order to be true.

A little thought will show that this assumption is wrong. We need only consider the familiar words of the first and second verses of the Twenty-third Psalm:

The LORD is my shepherd, I shall not want.
He makes me lie down in green pastures;
he leads me beside still waters;
he restores my soul.

Jews and Christians for centuries have sensed the profound *truth* of these verses, but no one with any sense thinks that the psalmist was a sheep, or that God feeds us grass!

"But," the objection comes, "that's poetry!" Or perhaps even, "That's *just* poetry." Well, poetry is not *just* something. It can be a way of conveying truth, although often not the kind of truth given by an accurate snapshot or newspaper article. And in any case, a good deal of the Bible, not only in the Psalms but throughout, is poetry. Relegating poetry to second class status cuts big pieces out of Scripture.

Let's look at another example. In the tenth chapter of Luke, a lawyer asks Jesus, "What must I do to inherit eternal life?" Part of the answer is from Leviticus 19:18, "You shall love your neighbor as yourself." But the lawyer, "wanting to justify himself," demands, "And who is my neighbor?"

Jesus presumably could have given some sort of legal definition of "neighbor." Instead, he tells a *story*: "A man was going down from Jerusalem to Jericho and fell into the hands of robbers ..." At the end of the story about the Good Samaritan, Jesus asks which of the three travellers who encountered the wounded man was his neighbor. The lawyer has to give the obvious answer, "The one who showed him mercy." Jesus then concludes, "Go and do likewise."

This parable does not seem as precise as a legal definition of "neighbor." But it conveys much better the meaning of "You shall love your neighbor as yourself" than any such definition.

Now is Jesus' story "true"? There is no reason to think that he is recounting some series of events which had actually happened. The story of the Good Samaritan is not something which we expect to find recorded on a police blotter in Jericho. Whether or not the events really took place is irrelevant to the bearing of the story on the question, "Who is my neighbor?" Jesus is using fiction to convey truth, as he does in other parables. The use of stories in this way is very widespread: Nathan told a story about a ewe lamb to bring home to King David the unpleasant truth about himself (2 Samuel 12:1-7).

This should not suggest that the Bible does not contain any material which is historically accurate. One example of such material is the so-called "succession narrative," 2 Samuel 9-20 and 1 Kings 1-2, which tells of the intrigues and struggles which resulted in Solomon's succession to the throne of his father David. This account (which happens to contain Nathan's parable) was probably set down by someone who had access to a great deal of first-hand information about the things which had happened, and who was interested in describing them accurately.

The Bible contains real historical material about a real people of Israel in Palestine some three thousand years ago. That history reaches its climax in Jesus of Nazareth who "suffered under Pontius Pilate," a Roman governor whose tenure we can date. The Book of Acts and the letters of Paul are sources which help us to understand the early spread of Christianity in the Mediterranean world. The Bible also contains descriptions of the physical world which are to be understood as in a sense scientific material, such as statements about the geography of Palestine.

But the Bible contains other literature besides accounts of "history as it really happened" and physical descriptions. In it we can find poetry, short stories, legends, laws, and liturgies. Furthermore, sometimes historical material in the Bible is edited to make a theological point. We can see that from the different ways in which the Gospel writers sometimes tell the same basic story about Jesus in order to emphasize things about him which are of interest to them.

For the purpose of the Bible is not to recount events or describe the world simply for the sake of historical or scientific accuracy. Psalm 148:4 calls on the "waters above the heavens" to praise God. There are no literal "waters above the heavens," waters of a cosmic ocean above the vault of the sky which fall as rain upon the earth when "the windows of the heavens" are opened (Genesis 7:11). The psalmist is using a model of the universe common in the ancient Near East to express the belief that all of nature is to praise its creator. Chanting this psalm in church does not commit us to that model as an accurate scientific description of the world.

We should not think that only ancient scientific descriptions can be out of date. Until the beginning of the twentieth century many scientists thought that space was filled with a peculiar material, the "luminiferous aether," and that light waves travelled through the aether as sound waves travel through air or water. A hymnwriter of that time might have sung about the aether resounding with God's praises. Einstein's relativity theory, however, has made the aether as obsolete as the waters above the heavens.

The fundamental purpose of Scripture is to tell people of God's purpose for the world and God's relationship with the world. In the Old Testament, that is focused in the story of Israel. In the New Testament, Israel's story culminates in Jesus, and in his death and resurrection. It points forward toward God's goal, to bring "all things" together in Christ (Ephesians 1:9-10). All the types of literature in the Bible should be seen in connection with that central theme if we are to grasp their deepest meaning.

We may seem to have strayed from our topic of science and religion. Let's turn then to part of the Bible which is certainly important for that topic, the first two chapters of Genesis.

The first chapters of Genesis contain two accounts of the creation of the world and of humanity. The first is the seven day account (six days plus the Sabbath) which extends from Genesis 1:1 through the middle of 2:4. (As in this case, the chapter and verse divisions of the Bible sometimes occur in awkward places. These divisions are much later than the original text and shouldn't be taken too seriously.) The second account, in which God places humans in the Garden of Eden, begins with the second half of 2:4 and continues through the end of that chapter.

There are several clues which indicate that there are two different accounts here. One thing which first suggested this to scholars is that different terms for the creator are used: In the first account it is simply "God" ('elohim in Hebrew) whereas in the second it is "the LORD God" (yhwh 'elohim). The orders of creation of living things also differ. In Genesis 1 we have plants — sea animals and birds — land animals — male and female humans, while in Genesis 2 the order is male human — plants — land animals and birds — female human (with no mention of sea life).

If we step back and look at the accounts as a whole, we see more general differences. In the first, God creates by sovereign commands: "Let there be...." In the second, God gets down into the dirt to make the first human. The backdrop in Genesis 1 is water, while in Genesis 2 it is desert.

These two creation accounts cannot really be "harmonized" as historical or scientific descriptions. They simply are too different. The sequence of events in Genesis 2 will not fit into the order of Genesis 1. Many attempts to bring the two accounts together assume without further thought that the sequence of events was that of the creation week in the first account, and then try to fit all of Genesis 2 into that sequence, but such a procedure doesn't respect the integrity of the second account.

This suggests that we should not try to read both accounts as chronological descriptions of events which happened in the earth's past. This conclusion follows from *internal* evidence — that is, from comparing different parts of the Bible with one another. There is also *external* evidence from comparison of the biblical accounts with our scientific knowledge of the world. The fact that there is an ocean above the sky in 1:7, as in Psalm 148, is one indication of this.

The use of "external" evidence, material outside the Bible, to help determine the meaning of the biblical text, might at first sound disturbing. We might wonder what has happened to the idea that "scripture alone" is to be the source of doctrine. But the belief that teaching is to be based on the Bible cannot mean that we are forbidden to look outside the Bible to interpret its meaning. In order to learn Hebrew and Greek to read and translate the Bible, people use secular textbooks and refer to pagan authors for information about how words are used. We use the science of geography to understand the settings of biblical accounts. Only we must be careful that we do not let ideas from external sources *control* our understanding of Scripture.

What we have said about Genesis 1 and 2, on the basis of both internal and external evidence, does *not* mean that the Genesis accounts are "wrong" or "untrue" or that they "contradict one another." People may come to those conclusions if they insist that everything in Genesis must be read as historical or scientific. But as we have seen, there is no need to make such an assumption. We can read the creation accounts for what they are, fundamentally religious statements about God as the creator of the world and the world's relationship with God. There is more than one account because biblical writers looked at belief in God as creator from different standpoints within the basic faith that the God of Israel is the one true God. The fact that we have four Gospels rather than just one is an indication of the same type of richness in presenting the story of Jesus.

We do not read the Genesis creation accounts as we would read articles by modern scientists or historians. That does not mean that they have nothing to do with our planet earth. They are not stories of some mythical world beyond our space and time, but religious statements about the world in which we live. In Genesis 2:10-14, four rivers flowing from Eden are named, and we can identify at least two of these, the Tigris and Euphrates. That is enough to show that the world described there is our world, though there is little point in trying to use this information to locate the Garden of Eden on a map.

We apparently have two different creation accounts, and the integrity of each should be respected. The question of who wrote these accounts is another issue. The traditional Jewish and Christian view is that the first five books of the Bible, including Genesis 1 and 2, were all written by Moses. Many modern biblical scholars think that while the traditions behind this part of the Bible may go back to Moses, the texts which we have were written and edited by others in later centuries. The first creation account probably dates to a time around that of the Babylonian exile in the sixth century B.C., while the second is earlier, perhaps from the tenth century B.C. during King Solomon's reign. But even if (as seems unlikely) Moses wrote both accounts, there are still two of them. They are written from different viewpoints and emphasize different aspects of creation.

Our purpose in this chapter has been to give some guidelines for reading the Bible and to warn against a common error. We have not said very much about the content of the creation stories. The following chapters, on cosmology and evolution, will have more to say about that.

But there is one more aspect of the creation stories which should be brought out at this point. Those stories are not just about the past, but are oriented toward the future and God's goal for creation. The first account concludes with the *Sabbath*, the day of rest. The observation of the Sabbath became for the Jews more than simply a weekly festival: It is a celebration in anticipation of the coming Kingdom of God, "the Bride Shabbat." In the Gospels, the reason that so many of Jesus' healings are performed on the Sabbath is that they were signs that the Kingdom of God was breaking into the world. That idea is still preserved in a medieval hymn by Peter Abelard:

> *Oh, what their joy and their glory must be,*
> *Those endless Sabbaths the blessed ones see!*
> *Crowns for the valiant, to weary ones rest;*
> *God shall be all, and in all ever blest.*[1]

The second creation story does not have the Sabbath. It concludes instead with the joining of man and woman in marriage, the beginning of human community. In the New Testament, the Letter to the Ephesians refers to the language of Genesis about the joining of husband and wife as "a great mystery" which refers to "Christ and the church" (Ephesians 5:32).

Any text of the Bible is part of the whole. Each part should be read carefully on its own terms to learn what the original author meant to communicate. But we do not have the deepest meaning of a text until we see its significance in the context of all of Scripture — and that is really the task of a lifetime.

Topics For Discussion

1. Psalm 104 is another biblical text about creation. What ideas about creation would we have if we concentrated on this psalm rather than the first two chapters of Genesis?

2. A t-shirt popular among scientists has the inscription, "And God said," followed by Maxwell's equations of electromagnetism which describe light waves, and concluding with "And there was light." Is this consistent with Genesis 1:3? Does it replace the statement in Genesis?

3. Carefully read and compare the three accounts of Jesus' temptation in Matthew 4:1-11, Mark 1:12-13, and Luke 4:1-13. How are they similar and how are they different? What kinds of texts are they?

---

1. *Lutheran Book of Worship* (Augsburg, Minneapolis, 1978), Hymn # 337, v. 1.

Chapter 7

The Origin Of The Universe

In this chapter we will explore the belief that the entire universe depends upon God. This includes the idea that the universe had a beginning at some point in time, though our interest is not limited to such a temporal origin. A major biblical text for our study, though it is not the only relevant one, will be the first creation account of Genesis. From a scientific standpoint, the main field of interest is physical cosmology, the study of the universe as a whole.

The basic biblical teaching about creation is that God is the *sole* creator of the universe: All things ultimately depend for their existence upon God alone. This is the essential meaning of the doctrine of "creation out of nothing." In Genesis 1, God does not have any helpers, and there is no pre-existing material which God has to wrestle into shape. Nothing puts up any resistance to God. When God speaks, it is done.

Scholars have debated whether or not that is what the first verses of Genesis mean. The traditional reading of the King James Version is "In the beginning God created the heaven and the earth." This suggests an absolute beginning. Some modern versions, such as TEV, have "In the beginning, when God created the universe, the earth was formless and desolate...." This suggests the existence of unformed material with which God would work.

We don't read Genesis 1 in isolation, but as part of the whole biblical story. In Isaiah 45:18 we read,

> For thus says the LORD,
> who created the heavens
> (he is God!),
> who formed the earth and made it
>   (he established it;
> he did not create it a chaos,
>   he formed it to be inhabited!):
> I am the LORD and there is no other.

And in Romans 4:17, Paul speaks of God as the one "who gives life to the dead and calls into existence the things that do not exist." In the context of the whole of Scripture we see that the first way of reading Genesis 1:1 is right: Creation is by God alone. The doctrine of creation out of nothing is not first of all a philosophical statement about nothingness and being, but about God as ultimate reality.

In Genesis 1, God creates by his *word*: "Let there be ..." For the prophets of Israel, who received and proclaimed God's word, that word was more than mere information. It *did* things — "Is not my word like fire, says the LORD, and like a hammer that breaks a rock in pieces?" (Jeremiah 23:29). The creation of the world is part of that activity of the word. And in the Gospel of John, Jesus is identified as the creative Word of God:

> *In the beginning was the Word, and the Word was with God, and the Word was God. He was in the beginning with God. All things came into being through him, and without him not one thing came into being ... And the Word became flesh and lived among us, and we have seen his glory, the glory as of a father's only son, full of grace and truth.* — John 1:1-3a, 14

There is tremendous richness in those verses. They echo Genesis 1, with its picture of God speaking the world into being. But the identification of the Word with Christ means that the Word is God's *personal* agent of creation, the same one in whom God was revealed when he "became flesh."

And there is still more that we can learn from a study of the opening verses of John's Gospel. The Greek word *logos* which is used here is translated as "Word" in most English versions. But *logos* can also have the sense of "reason" — it is, for example, the root of the English word "logic." This suggests that there is rational pattern underlying the universe, so that the world makes sense. That idea is very important in connection with scientific attempts to understand the universe in rational terms.

The creation account of Genesis 1 echoes with the refrain, "And God saw that it was good," coming to a climax with the statement that "everything" that God had made was "very good" (Genesis 1:31). Some religions have thought that the physical world was evil or an illusion, but the Bible insists upon its goodness. Among other things, this means that it is worth studying, and that the information which we gain from such study is reliable. (Thus the argument which is sometimes made, that God created the world just a few thousand years ago but made it look billions of years old, should be rejected. It would mean that God created the universe as a gigantic hoax.) The scientific study of the world can give us genuine knowledge about reality.

Scientific cosmology is the branch of that study which deals with the universe as a whole. What can it tell us about the structure and development of the universe?

We have already mentioned a couple of the basic discoveries of cosmology in the twentieth century. First, the universe is very large. The region which we can observe stretches out to distances of at least ten billion light years in all directions. (If we model the sun by a one-inch ball, the earth would be a dot .01 inch in diameter, nine feet from the sun, the nearest star would be 460 miles away, and the galaxy would be 10,000,000 miles across.) Such dimensions are humbling for us, but the fact that the universe is vastly larger than our planet was known to ancient Greek astronomers.

What is perhaps more surprising is that the universe is not static and unchanging. The systematic shift of galactic light toward the red end of the spectrum led Hubble in 1929 to the discovery that the galaxies are receding from one another, and the greater the separation between two galaxies, the faster they are moving apart. The entire universe is expanding.

Our knowledge of the universe of galaxies has grown tremendously since Hubble's work, in large part because of the space telescope named in his honor. But there is still a great deal that we don't understand, such as the ways in which galaxies form and evolve. The very bright *quasars* which we see at great distances are probably related to early phases of galaxies.

The expansion of the universe had already been anticipated by Einstein's general relativity theory, which described gravitation in terms of space-time curvature. Einstein's equations showed that the simplest types of curved space which serve as models of the universe could not remain at rest, but must expand or contract with time. Einstein originally resisted this conclusion because he (like almost everyone else at the time) thought that the large-scale aspect of the universe was unchanging and modified his equations to make this possible.[1] But with Hubble's discovery, it was seen that Einstein's original theory provided the tools which were needed to describe a universe which expands and which *might* eventually stop expanding and begin to contract.

If all the galaxies are expanding away from one another, it seems natural to conclude that in the past they were closer together. If we could go farther and farther back in time, we would see them packed closer and closer together. Eventually the material of the galaxies and their stars would be merged together in a single hot, dense cloud of gas which would be hotter and denser as we went farther back in time. The picture emerges of a cosmic explosion at some time in the past, an explosion which involved the entire universe. This explosion has come to be called the *big bang*, and the theory describing it is of course the big bang theory.

This is in some ways a simple picture, but we should not imagine that it is entirely common sense. Our tendency is to picture the big bang as a huge explosion *in space* — that space already existed and the material from the big bang flew out into it. But that is not the way Einstein's theory describes things. That theory links matter closely with space-time, so that not only matter but space itself expands. There is "more space" — that is, a greater number of cubic light years — now than there was billions of years ago.

Connected with this is the fact that in Einstein's theory there is no place "outside the universe." There is no point in space from which one could view the whole universe as an external observer. The universe may be infinite in extent, in which case there is clearly no outside: As far as you go, there would still be matter. Or the universe may be finite but, because of the curvature of space, without any boundary. We may think of the way in which the surface (not the interior) of the earth is finite in extent, a certain number of square miles, but is closed on itself and has no boundary. The corresponding situation for a finite universe is difficult to imagine because it is like the three-dimensional surface of a four-dimensional sphere. But even though we can't picture such an entity, it can be described mathematically.

How long ago did the big bang take place? It is difficult to get a precise answer to that question because it depends on accurate measurements of distance to remote galaxies, and several factors complicate these measurements and their interpretation. Thus the value given for "the age of the universe" has varied a good deal since Hubble's original discovery. We can be reasonably safe today if we give a value between ten and fifteen billion years.

We have spoken of this model of a cosmic explosion as a "natural" inference from the expansion of the universe. But is it really true? Are there other explanations for the recession of the galaxies which Hubble discovered? One very influential competitor of the big bang theory should be mentioned, especially because of the conclusions which some people drew from it for the doctrine of creation.

We said earlier that if we could go back in time, we would see the galaxies closer and closer together. In saying that, we were assuming that the amount of energy, and thus matter, in the universe is constant. Proponents of the *steady state* theory pointed out that we don't really have evidence that energy is conserved over vast stretches of time and space. Perhaps matter is somehow continually coming into existence, in such a way as to keep the average density of matter in the universe constant. Then the separation of the galaxies would be accompanied by appearance of new matter which would condense into new galaxies to fill the space created by the expansion. The universe would continually expand yet continually present the same overall appearance — hence the name "steady state."

It is easy to see how such a theory could be drawn into science-religion discussions. If the universe has existed forever then it might be argued that there was no creation. The universe never would have passed through a very hot, dense state, and there would have been no initial cosmic explosion. Alternatively, one might say that creation is now described by science. (Fred Hoyle's form of the theory made use of a "creation field" to explain the continual production of matter.) But whether one agreed with such conclusions or not, the steady state idea was a legitimate scientific theory which had to be evaluated in the light of observations.

And observations did eventually settle the debate between the big bang and the steady state in favor of the big bang. If there was a big bang, there should be radiation left over from the early stages of cosmic evolution when temperatures were very high. This radiation would now be cooled down considerably and shifted to longer wave lengths, but it should still be detectable. In 1965 the residue of this "primeval fireball" was found. Wherever in the sky we point our instruments, we find a background of microwave radiation with a temperature about three degrees above absolute zero. Observations made since 1965 have shown that this corresponds in detail with the radiation expected from the early universe.

When we detect the microwave background, we are looking back to a time when the universe was only about half a million years old. An analogy may help us appreciate the meaning of that. Suppose that we are now at noon of the cosmic day which began at midnight with the big bang. When we observe a galaxy which is receding at half the speed of light, we are seeing it as it was at about 6:30 a.m. The most distant quasar we can observe is at a few minutes after 1 a.m. And the microwave background? When we detect it, we are getting a signal from about one and a half *seconds* after midnight. In other words, we are looking back over about 99.997 percent of the history of the universe.

And we can detect signals of a different type from even earlier. In the hot, dense conditions in the first minutes of the big bang (in real time, not our analogy), nuclear reactions would have taken place. The light atomic nuclei formed by these reactions are fossils from the big bang. Theory predicts that about three-quarters of the mass of atoms in the universe should be hydrogen and one quarter helium, and that is found to be the case. We believe that the heavier elements (including carbon, which is essential for life) were formed later by fusion reactions in the interiors of stars. These processes are still going on today.

So the big bang really seems to have happened, and we can probe back into its first minutes. Scientists continue to look for evidence from even earlier epochs, when the basic physical interactions and elementary particles took the form that they now have. A theory of "quantum gravity," a combination of Einstein's general relativity and quantum theory, may even be able to explain how space-time and matter themselves originated in the first tiny fraction of a second when the entire universe we now see occupied a volume less than that of a present-day atomic nucleus.

Can such a scientific program possibly be compatible with belief in divine creation? If this idea of explaining the present-day universe in terms of processes which went on in the big bang is true, what sense can we make of the claim that "in the beginning *God* created the heavens and the earth"?

Here it is important to recall our discussion in Chapter 5. We said that God is the creator *today*, working through natural processes, and that faith is needed to see God (and not just the forces of nature) operating. But that is not just true today. It was true five centuries ago when Luther wrote the Catechism, and three thousand years ago when the people of Israel prayed for healing. Since the same natural processes seem to have been operating since the big bang, it makes sense to argue that God also has been working through them since then. Belief that God formed the light atomic nuclei by fusion reactions in three minutes after the cosmic expansion began is the same type of thing as believing that God causes grain to grow today.

The procedure we are following is similar to that used by scientists in their study of the universe. Science begins by trying to understand what goes on in our own small region of space and time, and then tries to extend that understanding out in space and back in time. We are doing the same thing with our understanding of how God acts in the world. There is no reason in principle to stop this effort at any particular moment in the past. It may be that God has called space-time and matter into being through the natural processes described by quantum theory and relativity. If this is the case, then God makes things make themselves, and by so doing conceals the divine action from our direct observation. To put it in another way, God creates the tools with which God works.

It is possible to give a sketch of the type of theory which might explain the origin of matter. Einstein showed that mass and energy are equivalent. The energy of a piece of a matter is positive, but the gravitational attraction between two bodies is described by a *negative* energy. If a number of particles came into being in such a way that their gravitational energy just cancelled their positive energy, there would be no violation of the law of conservation of energy, for the total energy would always be zero. This rather crude model doesn't prove that such a process could happen, but it does show that it is not simply impossible.

But to speak of God creating through the tools which God has made does not explain why God created *those* tools and not others. Science does not tell us why one set of rational laws and not another describes the universe, or why the particular pattern embodied in our universe is a reality. We must see creation of this rational pattern as basic for the creation of the universe itself. A Christian understanding of creation will see the source of this pattern as Christ, the *logos* or Reason of the universe. The letter to the Colossians (1:17) says that "he himself is before all things, and in him all things hold together."

The description to this point gives a picture of a universe with a beginning in time, some ten to fifteen billion years ago. Stephen Hawking has suggested a different view. Working with a quantum version of Einstein's gravitational theory and using an ingenious mathematical trick, he and James Hartle developed a model of a universe with no temporal beginning. Both space and time are represented on the surface of a multi-dimensional sphere. The time "$t = 0$" is not fundamentally different from other times, for all points on a sphere are equivalent. This universe does not come into being but "just is." This would seem to conflict with the idea of God's originating the universe "in the beginning."

We need to remember that what theorists like Hawking do is to create "models" of possible universes which are possible in the context of certain theories. These models may not necessarily be accurate descriptions of the way the universe actually is. In fact, the interest of the model may lie more in helping to understand the theory than in contributing directly to knowledge of the universe we inhabit. Nevertheless, even the possibility of a universe without boundaries in space *or* time deserves some reflection.

It is easy to slip into speaking of the universe as having a beginning "in time." From a theological standpoint that is inaccurate. Saint Augustine said that God "did not create the universe *in* time but *with* time." Time is part of God's creation, which means that God intended a world with change and history.

If the universe had no beginning, we would have to speak of creation as an *eternal* dependence of the universe upon God. As we noted at the beginning of this chapter, "creation out of nothing" means that ultimately God is the sole source of being of everything. God is always the creator — in past, present, and future. We will take up some of the issues of a cosmic future in later chapters. But now we need to turn our view to another aspect of the universe — the emergence and development of life.

Topics For Discussion

1. We sketched a model with the sun represented by a one-inch ball to give an idea of the size of the universe. What does the fact that the cosmos is vastly bigger than the earth tell us about the value or importance of our planet? What other factors might be taken into account?

2. The astronomer Robert Jastrow ended a book about the big bang theory and religion in this way:

> *For the scientist who has lived by his faith in the power of reason, the story ends like a bad dream. He has scaled the mountains of ignorance; he is about to conquer the highest peak; as he pulls himself over the final rock, he is greeted by a band of theologians who have been sitting there for centuries.*[2]

Is this an accurate picture of the relationship between scientific cosmology and theology?

3. Why are cosmologists content with describing the universe from the first few seconds onward, without trying to get all the way back to the very beginning?

4. Discuss the statement which was referred to at the beginning of the first chapter, that observation of details of the microwave background radiation shows us "the face of God."

---

1. Einstein added a "cosmological term" to his equations. This is effective only over very great distances and amounts to a new force of repulsion in addition to ordinary attractive gravity. Einstein dropped this after Hubble's discovery but recent observations suggest that it should be retained. It provides a way of harmonizing the ages of some star clusters with the time elapsed since the beginning of cosmic expansion.

2. Robert Jastrow, *God and the Astronomers* (Warner, New York, 1980), pp. 105-106.

Chapter 8

Evolution And Creation

It is no secret that religious questions raised by the theory of evolution have been hotly debated. For some people this is *the* question which decides whether or not a person is a Christian. It's true that there are difficult issues here, but belief in divine creation does not rule out acceptance of evolution as a scientific theory. A person may conclude that a careful reading of Genesis excludes evolution, or that scientific evidence doesn't support it. But no one should reject evolution because of a mistaken idea that it is automatically opposed to belief in creation.

Again we emphasize a point we have made previously: God can be understood as the one who creates by working through natural processes which God has created. (As it is sometimes put, God "makes things make themselves.") Whether or not there *are* natural processes which could cause certain things to happen is for science to determine.

We turn again to the first chapters of Genesis to begin a theological discussion of the origin of life. One aspect of the creation account of Genesis 1 which is often not emphasized is that it describes the creation of living things as being *mediated*. That is, God does not simply have living things appear from nothing, but commands the materials of the world which God has created to "bring forth" life.

> *Then God said, "Let the earth put forth vegetation: plants yielding seed, and fruit trees of every kind on earth that bear fruit with the seed in it." And it was so ... And God said, "Let the waters bring forth swarms of living creatures, and let birds fly above the earth across the dome of the sky." So God created the great sea monsters and every living creature that moves, of every kind, with which the waters swarm, and every winged bird of every kind. And God saw that it was good ... And God*

said, "Let the earth bring forth living creatures of ev-
ery kind: cattle and creeping things and wild animals
of the earth of every kind." And it was so.
— Genesis 1:11, 20-21, 24

The picture we have here is of God giving the material of the world the ability to produce life in accord with the divine command.

There is an emphasis on stability: Plants and animals are to reproduce "after their kind." We cannot, however, simply equate the word "kind" with the modern concept of "species." For a biologist, a species is "an isolated breeding population" — a class of organisms which can produce live offspring by breeding within that class but not with organisms outside that class. The Hebrew word which is translated "kind" might mean much larger classes than that in this account.

We should not make the mistake of thinking that the biblical writers had anything like a modern theory of evolution in mind. But the picture of mediated creation in Genesis 1 opens the way for some sort of understanding of development of living things by natural processes.

What about human beings? Their creation on the sixth day is set apart from the creation of the other land animals, and nothing is said about the earth bringing them forth. But if we turn to the second creation story we find the picture of earthly origin intensified. There God created the first human "from the dust of the ground, and breathed into his nostrils the breath of life; and the man became a living being" (Genesis 2:7). The human is made from the material of the earth and is alive because God gives this earth creature the gift of life.

Humanity is not unique in this regard. Trees and animals are also made "out of the ground" (Genesis 2:9 and 19). And other animals are alive because of the "breath" or "spirit" of God. In Psalm 104, after speaking of human beings together with storks and lions and other living things, the psalmist says:

When you hide your face, they are dismayed;
when you take away their breath, they die and return to
their dust.

When you send forth your spirit, they are created;
and you renew the face of the ground.

— Psalm 104:29-30

The uniqueness of human beings in the creation stories of Genesis lies in their being entrusted with special responsibilities and privileges. These require that they also have special abilities — foremost among these being the ability to receive God's communication, to know God's will and to do it, as in Genesis 1:26-29 and 2:15-17.

We see then that while the creation accounts of Genesis do not "teach evolution," they are open to scientific theories which describe evolutionary development. Furthermore, the repeated emphasis of the first account on the goodness of creation indicates that creation is *reliable,* in the sense that we can get true answers about its nature and history if we study the world honestly and intelligently. This means that we ought to be able to learn about the history of life on earth by studying the earth.

The basic idea of theories of evolution is that there have been gradual changes in species over long periods of time, so that the species which exist today are not those which populated the earth in the distant past. This means also that there should be relationships between organisms of different species.

There is evidence to support both these aspects of evolutionary theory. As we noted earlier, the fossil remains in different strata of rock do show that the organisms which lived millions of years ago differed in major ways from those today. *Jurassic Park* notwithstanding, there are no dinosaurs alive today. But a hundred million years ago, when the dinosaurs were flourishing, the mammals were an apparently insignificant group of small animals. As we look at deeper strata, we find even more radical differences.

It should not be thought that the fossil record is complete. In order to be fossilized, an animal or plant must die in a place where its remains will be buried in a material in which they, or their impression, will be preserved. The rock which is produced when this material is subjected to pressure must then remain uneroded, and of course we have to *find* the fossil. So it is largely a matter of

73

chance that fossils are preserved. The fossil record is not a complete history of life on earth, but more like pages torn randomly from an encyclopedia. Still, the study of fossils around the world during the past couple of centuries has been intensive enough that we have a good overall picture of the history of terrestrial life. And that history is one of changes in the types of living things which inhabit the earth. Roughly speaking, we see systematic changes as we go from lower and earlier strata to higher and more recent ones.

There is also evidence which indicates relationships between species which are alive today. The correspondence between anatomical structures, such as the bones of a bird's wing, a whale's flipper, and the human arm, is suggestive. Even more impressive are the similarities on the molecular level. Both the proteins of our bodies and the DNA which carries our genetic information are similar to those of other mammals, and the degrees of difference can be correlated with the closeness of evolutionary relationship. Even wider relationships are shown by the near-universality of the genetic code, the molecular sequences in DNA which signal for the construction of proteins from amino acids. The fact that this code is the same for virtually all living things on earth strongly suggests a common origin.

So the evidence suggests an evolutionary history. But how could this have happened? How could species change and eventually give rise to new species over the course of generations? Some plausible hypothesis must be given to answer that question if a theory of evolution is to be taken seriously.

If we may oversimplify somewhat, there are two basically different types of theories to explain how evolution could occur. The first, which is usually associated with the name of the French scientist Lamarck, is that organisms can pass on to their offspring the properties which they acquire during their lives. These properties can be enhanced generation after generation, until new forms emerge. For example, predators which make a greater effort to run down their prey will get faster and pass on that greater speed to their descendants.

That is an attractive idea because it fits in with the popular belief that we can improve the situations of ourselves and our

74

descendants by working hard. Species can earn survival, growth, and development through their own effort. From a theological standpoint, the idea might be described as a form of biological works righteousness.

Attractive or not, inheritance doesn't seem to work that way. Things that happen to tissues of the body of a plant or animal don't change the genetic information in the sex cells. The classic example is the blacksmith, whose children are not born with larger arm muscles because of their father's work. There are a few examples which seem to show some type of Lamarckian inheritance at work, but they probably don't play any significant role in evolution.

The other theory is that of *natural selection*, which was proposed separately by Darwin and Wallace. This is based on two observations. First, a given environment will not be able to support an unlimited number of organisms. Not all who are born will survive, and not all who survive will reproduce.

Second, in any species there will be variations among members — in size, speed, color, intelligence, and so forth. Some variations may be caused by mutations, molecular changes in the DNA of eggs or sperm due to radiation or chemical influence. Other variations may be simply statistical in nature, especially in small populations. Now because not all organisms can survive in the environment in which they find themselves, those whose variations make them best suited will be the ones most likely to survive and to have offspring to whom they will pass on their favorable properties. Thus natural selection is often referred to as "survival of the fittest."

"Fitness for survival" is not, however, an absolute quality. What is important is fitness for survival in a given environment. Good eyesight often gives a strong edge for survival — but not in a totally dark environment. Fish in Mammoth Cave have evolved from fish that could see to a state of hereditary blindness. We might be tempted to say that they have "degenerated," but that would miss the point. They are as well suited for survival in their environment as are sighted fish in environments in which it helps to be able to see.

There is also a limit to how well adapted to environmental *change* a species can be ahead of time. No species could have been "prepared" ahead of time for the asteroid impact sixty-five million years ago which filled the atmosphere with dust and smoke and caused temperatures to plummet and vegetation to die. The previously small and insignificant mammals were able to survive and the previously dominant dinosaurs died off.

Darwin and Wallace's original suggestion of evolution through natural selection was incomplete because at the time no one understood the mechanisms of heredity. Knowledge of these mechanisms began with Mendel's discovery of basic rules of genetics. During the twentieth century, tremendous increases in knowledge both of the genetics of populations and the molecular processes of heredity have made modern "neo-Darwinian" evolutionary theory quite comprehensive and successful.

Modern theories of evolution have not solved all the scientific problems connected with the origin and development of life. Those who oppose evolution sometimes overstate the difficulties, and those favoring evolution may minimize them. It is sometimes argued, for example, that the second law of thermodynamics rules out evolutionary theories. This law says that the amount of energy which can perform useful work in a closed system can never increase, and in general will decrease. It can be shown that this is equivalent to the statement that the atoms which make a system will never become more orderly, and in general will become more disordered. It might then seem that processes of ordering of atoms in living systems which evolution requires cannot take place.

But further reflection will show that this can't be the case. If it were, a sperm and ovum could never become a baby! Neither the organic molecules on the earth nor an embryo in the womb are closed systems. Both are receiving energy, from the sun and from the mother. Evolution cannot be denied just because of the second law of thermodynamics.

But there is a difference. The *information* for the developing embryo is already contained in the genetic material in the fertilized egg. For evolution of life from nonliving matter there is not a pre-existing store of genetic information which describes how atoms should be put together to make a living thing. In order to understand the origin of life scientifically we would have to explain how information and physical structure could develop together.

76

Thus we do not know how the first living molecular systems developed from non-living materials. This "origin of life problem" or "chemical evolution" is perhaps the biggest problem which still needs to be dealt with in the life sciences. Scientists speak about the formation of life in a "prebiotic soup," and a good deal of experimental and theoretical work has been done on this, but we do not yet have convincing answers. And if we knew how life began, we still would not know in detail how some of the very complex systems involved in living things at the cellular level could have evolved.

Some people, eager to find a place where God is "needed" in the world, seize upon these problems as evidence that science cannot explain the origin or development of life in all its complexity. It is true that scientists need to show more humility than they often have, and should not suggest that they know more than they really do. On the other hand, we should hesitate to postulate miraculous divine intervention because of our current state of ignorance. The "God" who is used to account for things which science can't explain may disappear as science makes further progress.

It is natural for us to be especially interested in the evolution of our own species. In fact, it is the consideration of human evolution which introduces us to some deep theological questions.

Human beings did not, as it is popularly said, "descend from apes." Chimpanzees, orangutans, and gorillas are the closest living relatives of our species *Homo sapiens*, but that means that we are descended from a common ancestral species a few million years ago. A great deal of fossil evidence for closer but now extinct species, the australopithecines, has been found in Africa, and it is generally believed that that continent is where humanity originated. The species in our direct line of descent seem to have been those now designated as *Homo habilis* and *Homo erectus*. We do not know just when our own species came into being, but we probably won't be too far off if we say that it was between a hundred and two hundred thousand years ago.

We can define our species, like any other, as an isolated breeding population. We can also give distinguishing characteristics of humanity — traditionally, rational thought and the use of tools.

Some apes do use very elementary tools, and some seem to be able to solve problems which require intelligence, but it is still clear that our abilities in these regards are of a quite different order. We don't know just how the unique human intelligence came into being. Undoubtedly it had to do with gradual growth in complexity of the brain, and especially the region of the cerebral cortex. But this gradual development may have reached a point at which reflective consciousness, the awareness of thought, suddenly "turned on." Paleontologist and theologian Teilhard de Chardin used the image of a pot of water being heated. The temperature increases slowly and nothing dramatic happens — until the boiling point is reached and something new emerges into being.

But what distinguishes human beings *theologically?*

We have already referred to this question in our look at Genesis, which does not speak directly about intelligence or ability to make and use tools. Both features are there indirectly, for without them human beings would not be able to "have dominion" and "till" and "keep" the garden (Genesis 1:26; 2:15). But what is distinctive about human beings in a religious sense is that they are given the ability to hear God's word and to trust and obey it. This requires intelligence, but it is more than rational thought. It is the ability to have faith, to trust, and to act out of that trust in God. Human beings have the capacity for personal relationships.

In the second creation account of Genesis, human beings are able to know God's will for them, and are called to obey God's will as an expression of faith.

> *And the LORD God commanded the man, saying, Of every tree of the garden thou mayest freely eat: But of the tree of the knowledge of good and evil, thou shalt not eat of it: for in the day that thou eatest thereof thou shalt surely die.* — Genesis 2:16-17, KJV[1]

It is assumed that the man and woman are able to obey this command — that it is possible for them not to sin. But of course, as we read in Chapter 3, they don't obey God. Sin enters the picture. And, especially from the way Paul deals with it in Romans 5, this is seen in many parts of the Christian tradition as the beginning of the human problem, as "original sin."

That is certainly not the end of the biblical story of humanity. In fact, we haven't even gotten to the most important part, which is that in Jesus of Nazareth God becomes human. That central aspect of the Christian faith has to be taken into account if we are to give adequate answers to theological questions about evolution. We will talk in greater detail about that in the next chapter. But there are some matters we can deal with at this point.

Maybe the most obvious question arises when we compare traditional descriptions of Adam and Eve in the western Christian tradition with what emerges from the scientific study of early humanity. Adam and Eve are often thought of as *perfect* creatures, not only sinless but with intelligence and other natural abilities far beyond those of their descendants. "An Aristotle was but the rubbish of an Adam," as one English writer put it.

Scientists can't know all the details about the intelligence and other abilities of early humans. But a good deal can be learned, from the remains of campsites with their stone tools and other debris, from the study of skulls and other bodily remains, and from the behaviors of our relatives in the evolutionary process. And none of these things gives any suggestion of superhuman gifts.

This may seem a serious problem. But if we take a closer look at the biblical creation stories, we will see that the picture of Adam and Eve as brilliant, beautiful, skillful people is greatly overstated. Genesis actually tells us almost nothing about their mental or physical abilities. And in fact, this picture of the first human beings has not been held by all Christians. There is a reason why this idea was spoken of above as part of "the western Christian tradition." The thought of the eastern church has generally been more moderate in this regard. The Greek theologian Irenaeus at the end of the second century saw Adam and Eve more like children than mature adults; and Athanasius, in the fourth century, thinks of them simply as being started on the road to union with God. They did not see the first human beings as created already in a state of perfection. That means that there would be some opportunity, and indeed need, for physical, mental, and spiritual development even if sin never came into the picture.

But we need to go deeper than that, for sin does come into the picture. The theological issue has to do fundamentally not with degrees of intelligence or other abilities but with trust in God and its lack, which is the basic sin. It is certainly not plausible to think of the first human beings as perfect, but Christian understandings of creation have generally understood that humanity was created *good*, in the sense of being able to have faith in God and not sin.

The problem here is that the evolutionary process would have left the first human beings with a considerable endowment of tendencies toward behaviors which would not have been sinful for their ancestors but would be for morally responsible agents. It would be a mistake to picture our prehuman ancestors as uncontrolled psychopaths: They were, after all, social animals to some degree like chimpanzees or gorillas today. But we know from those animals that there is sexual domination and aggression, violence, and theft. It seems very likely that human beings, even when their greater mental abilities came into play, would have had their brains "wired" for these same types of behavior. The distinctively human cerebral cortex and frontal lobes do not replace but are added to the parts of the brain which we share with other animals, the "reptilian" and the "old mammalian" brains, as they have been called.

This does not mean in the strict sense that human beings were *forced* to sin, but it does suggest that it would have been very hard for them not to. One way of making this distinction is to say that while sin is not "necessary," it is "inevitable."

For western Christians, that requires some serious rethinking of ideas about humanity. One way of starting that rethinking is to turn our attention from the past to the future. While beginnings are important, God's *purpose* for humanity also has to be kept in view.

The reader may have noticed that we have said nothing yet about one important idea concerning humanity which is introduced in the first creation story. "Then God said, 'Let us make humankind in our image, according to our likeness' " (Genesis 1:26a). The "image of God" has been understood as the thing which distinguishes humanity. But this image cannot be understood within the story of origins alone. It is also something which points toward the future, and we turn to that in the next chapter.

Topics For Discussion

1. People sometimes ask, "Do you believe in creation *or* evolution?" Is this helpful way of putting the question? Why or why not?

2. What are some of the reasons that evolution is such a controversial topic?

3. The suggestion is sometimes made that Genesis 1 can be thought of as an accurate scientific description of earth history if each day is considered to be millions of years long. Is this scientifically sound? Is it a useful approach to the interpretation of Scripture?

_____

1. This citation is from the King James Version because it conveys, as the NRSV does not, the emphatic note of the Hebrew: "Thou shalt *surely* die."

Chapter 9

A Human Universe?

Since its beginnings in the sixteenth century, modern science has seemed to be in a process of removing humanity from any important place in the universe. Copernicus moved the center of the planetary system from our earth to the sun, and evolution made *Homo sapiens* just one among a huge family of species which happened to have the right qualities for survival in certain circumstances. And the whole approach of science up to the beginning of the twentieth century assumed that what went on in the world didn't depend on whether or not anybody was watching things. It seemed to be a basically impersonal universe, one so big and so old that what happened to one species on one small planet couldn't be of much account in the whole picture.

Is it all just a matter of chance? Are there perhaps any reasons why the universe is so big and so old? Well, to begin with, the size and age of the universe seem to be related. Einstein's gravitational theory indicates that almost any possible universe must be expanding or contracting. Since the most distant things we can see will be moving close to the speed of light, a universe ten billion years old must extend outward about ten billion light years. An old universe will be big.

But do we just happen to be alive now when the universe is about ten billion years old? In order for us to be here at all, the universe had to expand and cool down enough for material to condense into galaxies and stars. Since the first generation of stars and any planets orbiting them would have contained only hydrogen and helium and no carbon, life could not yet have developed. In order for that to take place, those stars would have had to build up carbon, oxygen, and other elements by nuclear fusion in their interiors, and then, in the types of explosions which we observe near the end of stellar life, scatter those heavy elements through interstellar space. Eventually those materials could become part of a new generation of stars, some of which could have planets. Under the right circumstances, carbon-based life could come into being and evolve. As we saw in the last chapter, we don't really understand the processes by which the first life on earth developed, but it apparently did happen by the time the earth was about a billion years old. It took another three and a half billion years for intelligent life — us — to evolve on our planet.

Maybe some of those processes could have happened more quickly, and maybe not. But we can be fairly sure that intelligent life couldn't yet have evolved in a universe which was only a thousand or even a million years old. *If the universe weren't as old as it is, we wouldn't be here to observe it and ask questions about it!* The present age and size of the universe are necessary conditions for there to be intelligent observers of the universe.

Just speaking about the universe's age and size gives only a rough description of it. What about the finer details? Some of the most important properties of the universe are the strengths of the basic physical interactions, the gravitational and electromagnetic forces and the forces which hold the atomic nucleus together. The gravitational force, for example, is quite weak for objects on a human scale. Two people who weigh 150 pounds and are four feet apart will attract one another (gravitationally) with forces of about a millionth of an ounce. That seems to be a quite arbitrary value. Is there any reason why gravitation shouldn't be much stronger or weaker than that?

We can certainly imagine a universe with much stronger gravity. In such a universe, this force in the very early stages of the big bang would have quickly slowed the cosmic expansion, so that it would have stopped and been followed by a "big crunch" before there had been time for galaxies, stars, planets, and life to form. On the other hand, if gravity were a great deal weaker, the material of the universe would have thinned out too quickly for these structures to develop. In either case, life would not have come into being.

The situation for the other forces is similar. In the atomic nucleus there is balance between the attractive electrical forces which the protons exert on one another (since like charges attract) and the strong nuclear forces which hold them together. In some cases this balance is rather delicate. If it were disturbed slightly, the fusion reactions by which three helium nuclei combine to form carbon couldn't take place. That would result in a sterile universe, for without carbon there would be no life as we know it.

It seems then that there are a number of factors which happen to be just right for the development of intelligent life. (And since we are the only intelligent physical beings we know of at this time, we might as well say that these factors allow the development of humanity.) These "just right" properties have been called "anthropic coincidences" because they enable the human, the *anthropos* in Greek, to evolve. They may simply be amazing coincidences — or they may be more than that. The idea that there is some significance to these coincidences has been called the Anthropic Principle. Because different people interpret this idea in different ways, and some attach much more significance to their versions than do others, it might really be better to use the plural and speak of Anthropic Principles.

No one can argue with a version of the Anthropic Principle which simply observes that conditions in our universe allow the existence of intelligent life. After all, we are here. But stronger versions of this principle quickly become more controversial. We enter here into theories and interpretations which are hotly debated among scientists. They are not simply "science fiction" — we will discuss that in a later chapter — but neither are they well established theories like Einstein's relativity or the molecular basis of heredity.

These stronger versions of the Anthropic Principle claim not only that intelligent life *does* exist but that a possible universe *must* be one in which such life could come into being. They may go even further and say that intelligent life must indeed develop in order for the universe to exist. And some even argue that intelligent life cannot cease to exist once it comes into being, but will achieve greater and greater control of the cosmos.

How could it be that the universe *must* bring forth intelligent life in order to exist? Doesn't there have to be a universe in the first place in order for anything to develop within it?

One answer to those questions takes the form of a *participatory anthropic principle*. This is based on a view of the world suggested by quantum mechanics, in which the basic description of the world is in terms of probabilities. Since we actually do get definite results when we observe physical systems, these probabilities must in some way become certainties. How this happens is one of the crucial problems of quantum theory.

Suppose that we shoot a beam of electrons at an obstacle, so that half of them go in one direction and half in another. Quantum mechanics does not tell us definitely which path any one electron will take, but only that there is a fifty percent probability for it to go either way. Suppose now that we reduce the intensity of the beam, so that only one electron at a time strikes the obstacle. Quantum theory still tells us that there is a fifty-fifty probability for either path. But if we place detectors along the two paths to see which one the electron actually takes, one of those probabilities suddenly becomes 100 percent and the other becomes zero. What causes that change? In a radical departure from the belief that our minds can be cleanly separated from the rest of the world which we observe, some physicists suggest that it is the act of observation *plus our awareness of it* which causes this change from probability to certainty. If this is so, intelligent observers are necessary for the existence of any definite result and, ultimately, of the universe. The universe and observer enable one another's existence by mutual participation.

With such wide-ranging claims associated with the Anthropic Principle, it is scarcely surprising that many people see it as having religious, or anti-religious, significance. Some people, both Christians and atheists, reject the whole idea because it seems to them like a thinly disguised substitute for religion. On the other hand, some have quite clearly made the Anthropic Principle a basis for their religion. Physicist Frank Tipler, for example, has argued for an extreme version of the final Anthropic Principle in which God is to come into being as the climax of intelligent life at the big crunch when the universe finally collapses.

Those are extreme views. More modest understandings of the Anthropic Principle look upon it as material for a type of natural theology which we discussed in Chapter 3. One of the mainstays for natural theology has always been the so-called argument from design: Things in the world are marvelously designed, so there must be a Designer, and that Designer can be identified with God. Natural selection removed much of the force of this argument, for it claimed that the properties of living things could have arisen through the filtering process of the environment upon random variations. But the Anthropic Principle suggests that the argument from design can be applied not just to individual organisms or species, but to the whole universe. If the universe is finely tuned for the development of intelligent life, there must be a Tuner, God.

That seems to be a plausible argument, but it is not conclusive. There are other ways of explaining the fine tuning. One way, the so-called "many worlds interpretation" of quantum mechanics, seems even wilder than the idea that consciousness plays a role in making the results of observations definite. In our previous example of an electron striking an obstacle and having equal probabilities of travelling either of two paths, the many worlds interpretation says that both possibilities are realized! The universe "splits" when an observation is made, so that there is one world in which an electron was seen to take one path, and another world in which it took another. When we take into account all possible observations which can be made on physical systems, we see that "our" world would be only one of countless trillions of worlds, and that all the others differ in greater or lesser degree from the one we are aware of.

If all possible worlds exist as branches of a "multiverse," there will be worlds in which conditions are right for evolution of intelligent life, and in some of these intelligence *will* evolve. We simply happen to inhabit one of them instead of one of the vast number in which life is impossible. There is no need to appeal to any idea of a designer to explain this, since everything which is compatible with the laws of physics can be found in some branch of the multiverse.

The use of the Anthropic Principle as an argument from design is as valid as, and some would say more valid than, the idea of a multiverse of all possible worlds. It cannot be considered a *proof* that there is a creator, since there is an alternative — though bizarre — explanation for the anthropic coincidences. The design argument, in other words, may be seen as a "plausibility argument" which should gain a fair hearing for belief in a creator, but cannot make a definite case for such a creator.

The design argument tries to move from our observation of nature to knowledge of God. We can also go in the other direction, moving from God's revelation in Christ to nature. When we do that, we find other interesting connections between Christian theology and the Anthropic Principle. The letter to the Colossians speaks of Jesus as *the human for whom the universe was created.*

> *He is the image of the invisible God, the firstborn of all creation; for in him all things in heaven and on earth were created, things visible and invisible, whether thrones or dominions or rulers or powers — all things have been created through him and for him. He himself is before all things, and in him all things hold together.*
> — Colossians 1:15-17

Christ is the goal and purpose of creation as well as the agent of creation and the one who sustains creation.

As we have seen, some versions of the Anthropic Principle argue that humanity is a central feature of the universe, which could not exist without intelligent life. The Christian doctrine of the Incarnation, which comes at the question from a completely different direction, says that humanity indwelt by the Word of God, God Incarnate, is the reason for creation. The letter to the Ephesians speaks of God's "plan for the fullness of time, to gather up all things in him [Christ], things in heaven and things on earth" (Ephesians 1:10). The Anthropic Principle could be seen as a description of the setting for this doctrine, a requirement that the universe be one in which the Incarnation could occur. The Anthropic Principle certainly doesn't "prove" the doctrine of the Incarnation, but the two ideas do seem to illumine one another.

There is, however, much more involved here than might be obvious at first glance. For what we are talking about now is *God's participation in the evolutionary process.* There are several important conclusions that we could draw from that.

If God's purpose in creation is to bring "all things" into union with himself by becoming a participant in cosmic history, there is no need to insist that the development of our particular species was "hard wired" into the universe at the big bang. Presumably divine Incarnation would take place in an intelligent species, for it is not easy to see what could be meant by the *personal* union of God with a stone or tree. But there would be no need for that intelligent species to be the two-footed mammalian species *Homo sapiens* on planet earth. That means that there could be room for a good deal of chance in the whole evolutionary process, since it would not have to end up precisely with us.

But the intelligent species which did eventually arrive — at least on earth — was us. When "the Word became flesh" (John 1:14) it was as *Homo sapiens.* That means that special importance is attached to our species, but not that our species is picked out to the exclusion of others. Through the evolutionary process we are related to other earthly species, living and extinct. We are cousins of the apes and distant relatives of fish. And in becoming completely human, the Word of God takes on those relationships as well. That gives us a point to start in thinking about how all things may be brought into union with God through the Incarnation.

Just to speak of the Incarnation does not reveal the full depth of God's involvement with creation. "And being found in human form, he humbled himself and became obedient to the point of death — even death on a cross" (Philippians 2:7b-8). God shares in the suffering and dying of creation, a painful and humiliating dying. The passage from Colossians which we quoted earlier goes on to speak of this as the way in which God accomplishes the divine purpose for the cosmos.

> *He is the head of the body, the church; he is the beginning, the firstborn from the dead, so that he might come to have first place in everything. For in him all the fullness of God was pleased to dwell, and through him God was pleased to reconcile to himself all things, whether*

on earth or in heaven, by making peace through the
blood of his cross. — Colossians 1:18-20

One of the greatest difficulties which many people have had with evolution has to do with the idea of natural selection. That theory says that the development of life has come about through processes of scarcity, competition for resources, death, and extinction. We shouldn't overdo the image of "nature red in tooth and claw." The extinction of many species has come about through slow decline in birthrates rather than by bloody slaughter. Still, extinction is death. We are here in large part because many other species have perished. And the difficulty simply is, how can we picture a good God creating life through this process? Do we really want to say that God forces millions of generations of creatures through this relentless struggle and death in order to accomplish some purpose?

The whole problem of "justifying" God and of explaining "why bad things happen to good people" is a very old one. People as far back as the book of Job have been wrestling with it and often end up with about the same answer Job got from God: "You don't understand because you're not God." And to some extent we have to be satisfied with that.

But the cross provides at least a different way of looking at this question. We don't have to picture a God somewhere off in heaven forcing other creatures through the processes of natural selection without any cost to himself. In Jesus, God becomes a participant in that process *on the side of the losers in the struggle for survival* — because in the short term it is those who want to hold on to their power at all costs, Pilate and Caiaphas, who win. Jesus is rejected by the religious and political establishments and killed.

And Easter means that death doesn't have the last word. It isn't the end for humanity or for all creation. If it is really true that "all things" are reconciled to God through the cross of Christ, then there must be some way in which it holds a promise even for those species which have become extinct. There is hope for the dinosaurs.

The Anthropic Principle suggests that the *anthropos*, the human, has a central role in cosmic evolution. But in an evolutionary view, humanity cannot be separated from all the rest of the universe. We are here because of what happened to other species on earth to which we are related, and in a still larger view owe the form which our life has taken to the nuclear reactions which created our elements in stellar interiors billions of years ago. We are, as Carl Sagan used to say, "made of star stuff."

So the Anthropic Principle should not lead us to think that our view of the world can be exclusively *anthropocentric*, concerned only with human welfare. The science of ecology has shown us that we ourselves will suffer if we take such a narrow view, because the welfare of the human species is bound up with that of our environment. We turn to such concerns in the next chapter.

Topics For Discussion

1. Medieval theologians debated the topic, "Whether Christ would have come if humanity had not sinned." What biblical texts might be relevant to this question? Does our discussion in this chapter shed any light on it?

2. If you try drawing a person in a two-dimensional space like a sheet of paper, you'll see that the alimentary canal would divide the person in half, and that nerves from various parts of the body would intersect one another. Does this suggest anything about importance of the three-dimensional character of our space?

3. The child's question, "Will my cat go to heaven?" is sometimes treated rather condescendingly. How should it be dealt with in light of Isaiah 11:6-9 and Colossians 1:20?

Chapter 10

Religion And The Environment

A lot of attention has been given to the state of the environment during the past three decades. Items about global warming, pollution, the rain forests, and other environmental topics are in the news continually. The various dimensions of environmental issues have all involved some controversy. There have been disagreements on scientific issues such as global warming because they are very complex questions, requiring analysis of a great deal of data, taking into account a large number of factors, and often sophisticated computer modelling. The economic, political, and social aspects of environmental decisions have a strong impact on the patterns of our lives and our welfare, and so naturally evoke heated debate. And there has been religious controversy about environmental issues as well.

Part of that controversy can be traced to a short but influential 1967 article by historian Lynn White, "The Historical Roots of our Ecologic Crisis."[1] White argued that the environmental crisis — which was just beginning to come to public attention at the time — was due in large part to the way in which the Judaeo-Christian tradition had interpreted the creation stories of Genesis. In particular, the statement of Genesis 1:28 that humanity was to "have dominion" over nature had, he argued, led to the idea that nature was simply here for humanity's benefit, and that we could do with it whatever served our purposes. White recognized that there were Christians who had had a different view, such as Saint Francis of Assisi, but believed that their influence had been relatively minor.

Not surprisingly, many Christians have been unhappy and rather defensive about the idea that environmental problems can be laid at their door. But it does have to be admitted that damage to the environment has been caused, if not by the first chapter of Genesis, by the ways in which people have understood that chapter and the relationship which it points to between humanity and nature. What is needed is not simply pointing of fingers or refusal to accept blame, but an attempt to discern the type of relationship between humanity and the environment to which the Bible directs us.

Before we do that, however, we should perhaps explain what this has to do with our "science and religion" topic. This may not be clear because often "environmental theology" is discussed without any connection with the more general issues of creation and God's relationship with the world. But it is helpful to see such theology as part of the larger dialogue between science and religion.

In the first place, we need to know something about how different parts of the environment, including human beings, interact with one another. This is precisely what the science of ecology attempts to describe. But science is also involved because it has been the use of science-based technologies — power and transportation systems requiring sources of energy, chemicals used in agriculture, and so forth — which has given rise to environmental problems. In some cases wiser use of science-based technology may be the key to solving those problems, and in other cases we may need to limit our uses of technology. Either course of action requires some ability to predict its consequences.

Having said that, what does the Bible have to tell us about what our attitude and actions with respect to nature should be? We can set out a few basic position statements with some scriptural support. One always needs to be careful about citing individual Bible verses to prove something: It is always important to pay attention to the setting in which those verses occur, a setting which finally is all of Scripture, as we saw in Chapter 6.

First of all, the natural world which God has created is *good*. This is stated over and over in Genesis 1 and is affirmed in the New Testament in 1 Timothy 4:4. This goodness is more than just an abstract "rating" and does not mean only that things are good for us to use. God cares for all living things, as Sirach (Ecclesiasticus) 18:13 in the Apocrypha says: "The compassion of human beings is for their neighbors, but the compassion of the Lord is for every living thing." The fact that God sees creation as good means that it is worthy of our love and honor as well.

94

The world is good, but it is not God. The prophets of Israel struggled for centuries with various forms of nature worship, and Paul says in Romans 1:18-25 that worshiping and serving created things instead of their creator is the fundamental human sin. Thus forms of environmentalism which treat nature itself as divine are ruled out for Christians.

The concept of *covenant* is a central part of the biblical story: God establishes a covenant with those he chooses to bless. Important stages in this process are God's covenant making with Abraham and with the people of Israel at Mount Sinai. In Jeremiah 31:31-33 God promises a "new covenant," and this becomes a reality at the Last Supper when Jesus gives his disciples the cup as a "new covenant in my blood." But the first mention of covenant in the Bible is in the flood story. Before the deluge God promises a covenant with Noah (Genesis 6:18), and after the flood gives it a very broad scope. The covenant is with Noah and his descendants (Genesis 9:9), "with every living creature that is with you" (9:10), and with "the earth" (9:13). The whole earth is God's covenant partner.

As part of that partnership, God promises to make a covenant between human beings and animals (Hosea 2:18). And God's covenant with the people of Israel includes specific directives for care of the land (Leviticus 25:1-17). Today's agricultural science gives us techniques for such care which are more sophisticated than the procedure of letting land lie fallow which Leviticus prescribes, but the principle of care should remain the same.

The creation story of Genesis 2 makes it clear that human beings are part of the earth, and not pure spirits who have somehow become trapped in matter. But God also gives humanity a special position in creation, as texts like Psalm 8 and Luke 12:24 bring out. God cares for the ravens — but human beings are of more value to God than birds.

Human beings are to care for creation. We will discuss later the problems raised by Genesis 1:26, with its statement that humanity is to "have dominion" over the other creatures. Here we point out that this should be seen in connection with God's statement in the first part of the verse, "Let us make humankind in our image, according to our likeness." Part of this idea of the "image of God" is that humanity is to be God's representative in caring for the world. Thus we should act toward the world according to the pattern which God shows — a pattern of "compassion ... for every living thing." That pattern reaches its clearest expression in Jesus, for whom being Lord (in Latin, *dominus*) does not mean domination and exploitation, but service (Mark 10:45).

The image of God has sometimes been understood as having to do with the fact that human beings are *rational* animals. We might also speak of the human ability to do things, our tool-making capacity, in this connection. We *need* to be rational and have technical capabilities in order to be able to know how to care for the earth and to do it. Our skills don't just put us in a privileged position, but give us the ability to serve in ways that really will be helpful.

The second creation account speaks of humanity's calling in another way. The human is placed in the garden "to till it and keep it" (Genesis 2:15). This could also be translated "to serve and to keep it." The idea is again human care for the world which God has created. It is interesting that the same Hebrew verbs as in Genesis 2:15 are also used in Numbers 3:7-8 to describe the duties of the members of the tribe of Levi who are to care for Israel's sanctuary, where God was present for his people.

This hints at the idea that the care of the garden/earth has religious significance as the care of God's dwelling. This idea will be developed further in a later chapter, when we consider the view which the Bible gives us of the future. The New Testament is not as concerned as the Old with issues related directly to care for the land, but puts those issues in the context of God's ultimate purpose for creation.

The Bible often speaks in a favorable way about human technology. A verse such as Genesis 4:22 traces technology back to the early phases of the human race, and in Exodus 31:1-11 various crafts are inspired for the service of God's sanctuary. Biblical writers often use technological images such as architecture and agriculture (e.g., Jeremiah 1:4-10) and metallurgy (e.g., Malachi 3:2-3). On the other hand, the story of the tower of Babel (Genesis 11:1-9) is a warning against the pride which accompanies excessive trust in technology, a danger which is especially strong with military technology (e.g., Isaiah 31:1).

The Old Testament law also includes specific directions about care for nature. We've already seen that the land is to be given rest. The book of Deuteronomy places limits on what the Israelites can do with trees (20:19) and birds (22:6-7). As with care for farmland, the point for us is not so much the details of these commandments as the principle they embody: We are not to look just to our short term interests, but to the welfare of creation as a whole.

Leviticus 25 makes a close connection between care for the land and justice among human beings. There are also negative consequences for nature if justice is ignored, as the vision of the prophet Jeremiah (4:23-28) suggests. We know today that the reverse is true as well: Environmental damage can cause injustice among humans beings.

So the Bible as a whole enjoins care for the earth and responsible use of its resources. But what about the argument that the environmental crisis has been brought on because of the teaching of Genesis 1? Is that just a misunderstanding, or is there a real danger here?

"Let them have dominion" can — and often has — given people the wrong idea about humanity's relationship with nature when it is taken out of context. The Hebrew word translated "dominion" does by itself have a very strong sense. It carries the idea of "trampling upon," as an ancient conqueror might symbolically step on the necks of defeated enemies. But the effect of this language would be very different for an ancient Hebrew and for people in modern technological societies.

People in the ancient world were helpless against the forces of nature to an extent which is difficult for us to appreciate today. It was a common belief that people were slaves of the powers who ruled the world. That is the idea given in the Babylonian creation epic: Human beings are made to serve the gods and goddesses, to do the dirty work so that the deities don't have to soil their hands. In such a setting, the message that God intends human beings to "have dominion" over the earth would be a word of liberation. The idea that humanity actually could do the things to nature that our technology makes us capable of didn't occur to the people of Israel 3,000 years ago.

So the words of Genesis 1 have to be seen in their cultural and historical context. They must also be seen in the context of the rest of Scripture, which does give humanity a special place of honor in creation, but also gives us special responsibilities.

What we have done to this point is to set out some basic theological guidelines for our relationship with our environment. The Bible does not tell us the best ways to use — or not use — our technologies in order to carry out the commission to serve and keep the terrestrial garden as well as to act justly toward other people. We have to turn to scientists, engineers, and economists, rather than theologians, in order to answer practical questions about the real threats to the environment and what should be done about them. The fact that the universe does make sense, so that scientific study can understand it, can give us confidence in the belief that we can live responsibly in the world. At the same time, the complexity of our interactions with nature means that there may be disagreements between intelligent and honest people about how to do that.

There are some very simple and basic principles upon which intelligent people ought to be able to agree, however. In the first place, we are part of an interdependent system of which other species and the inorganic world are parts. The welfare of each species is connected with the welfare of other species. Just as evolutionary theory deals with the relationships among species over long periods of time, ecology deals with their relationships throughout a region of space over shorter time spans.

For ecological relations between organisms are not static. They change over the course of time, and over sufficiently long periods, the study of ecological relationships will merge into the study of evolutionary ones. While we are properly concerned about the destruction of species, we must remember that extinction has been a central part of the story of evolution for millions of years. We cannot and to some extent should not stop all extinctions. That may seem uncaring, like letting wildfires burn unchecked in national parks. But in the long run it may be the healthiest policy for the total ecosystem.

But before we absolve ourselves of the blame for the destruction of species because it's been going on for a long time, we must also recognize that the impact on the environment of our modern technological society differs in many ways from natural predation or disease. We can, and unfortunately have, poisoned waters, lands, and air with pesticides and other chemical products. There are good reasons for using such chemicals, but also destructive side effects.

Another fundamental reality is the finite character of our resources — land, clean water and air, fossil fuels, and others. While we cannot give an exact date, we know that the world will almost certainly run out of petroleum in the twenty-first century. That means that we will have to find, or do without, other sources of energy and the chemicals which are now produced from oil.

It is perhaps not too much of a stretch to see the finiteness of our resources as a symbol of our finite nature as creatures. Though we are to be representatives of God in caring for creation, we are not God. We do not have infinite power and unlimited resources. Our calling is to be faithful as finite and limited creatures, putting our trust not in our ability to do anything we want but in the unlimited love and faithfulness of the creator.

Topics For Discussion

1. People who oppose what they see as excesses of the environmental movement sometimes argue that if we believe in creation, we can trust that God will preserve the environment no matter what we may do to it. Do you agree? Why or why not?

2. Do observances such as Earth Day carry with them a risk of nature worship? If so, how can these dangers be avoided?

3. Do human beings have any moral obligations to non-human animals like dogs and horses? What about chimpanzees? Mosquitoes? Trees?

---

1. *Science*, 10 March 1967, p. 1203.

Chapter 11

Old Medicine And New

The issues which we discussed in the last chapter arise from the impact of our technology upon our external environment. As we saw, what happens to the rest of nature will also affect us, if only in indirect ways. Our technology also has direct impacts upon ourselves. That is the purpose of medicine — to improve our own lives. In the past, medical art and science was directed toward healing injuries and enabling people to recover from diseases. Today we also have the possibility of making deliberate improvements in human beings by altering their basic molecular structures. Both old and new medicine raise questions about God's role in the world and about the proper use of our abilities.

The type of work which we associate today with the medical profession is very ancient. Egyptian mummies bear the marks of surgical incisions — healed incisions, indicating that patients survived the operation, and that in some cases the surgery was successful. The Bible is aware of the work of physicians, and in one passage in the Apocrypha, Sirach 38:1-15, this work is given high honor. One of the co-workers of Saint Paul was "Luke, the beloved physician" (Colossians 4:14). Of course doctors weren't always able to heal, as Mark 5:26 notes.

We have emphasized throughout this book that God normally works with the physical processes of nature, which faith sees to be the instruments through which God is active in the world. That can also be said of the work of doctors, nurses, and other health professionals. As part of faith in God's creative and sustaining work, we can see God at work in their skills and in the medicines, surgery, radiation, diet, physical therapy, and other techniques which they use. As one Renaissance surgeon said of a patient, "I bandaged him. God healed him."

It is unfortunate, then, that Christians have sometimes thought that there is some contradiction between belief in God's healing power and the use of doctors and medicine. Some sects are strongly opposed to such means of healing. But to think that going to a doctor shows lack of faith in divine healing is exactly the same kind of thinking as the idea that a faithful Christian should sit at the table waiting for food to appear miraculously instead of going to the store to buy it!

The fact that Christians should use doctors and medicine doesn't mean that there is nothing distinctively Christian which should be done in cases of illness or injury. In our discussion of God's action in the world, we noted that this leaves room for God to take prayers into account, and prayer for healing is certainly appropriate. From very early times the Christian church has also had the practice of anointing the sick with oil, as we read in Mark 6:13 and James 5:14-15. This should not be thought of as an *alternative* to medicine. Olive oil itself was regarded as a medicine in the Bible, as in Isaiah 1:6 and Luke 10:34. We would regard this today as a very mild home remedy, and we of course have much more effective medicines. But oil can be regarded as a symbol for all medicines, so that the rite of anointing of the sick is an acted out form of prayer for healing through medical means. It does not take the place of medical science but asks for God's action through it. God may also heal miraculously, but it is no business of ours to specify how God is to work.

The understanding that God works through the processes of nature, processes which we are able to understand and make use of, answers most of the theological questions which might arise in connection with medicine. Most of the difficult questions which medical science poses for us today are *ethical* questions connected with new bio-medical technologies: "Should we or should we not use this particular technique in this situation?" or "Who should benefit from this new medical development?"

Many new bio-medical technologies and the ethical challenges which they raise were not dreamed of a few decades ago. Though we can't discuss all of these in detail, it may be helpful to list here some of the major things which bio-medical ethics needs to address. Some of the terms which may be unfamiliar will be explained in the following pages.

- Genetic counselling
- Genetic engineering (germ line therapy and somatic cell therapy)
- Cloning
- Fertility technologies (artificial insemination, *in vitro* fertilization, contraception, etc.)
- Pre-natal technologies (diagnosis, surgery, abortion, and so on)
- Informed consent for procedures
- Organ and tissue donation and transplants
- Allocation of medical resources and technologies
- Use and withdrawal of life support
- Euthanasia, suicide, and assisted suicide

Instead of looking at all of these (which would take a book in itself), let's consider some of the important concerns at the beginning, in the middle, and at the end of human life.

A great deal of attention has been given to developments in *genetic engineering* and *cloning*. Genetic engineering refers to modification of the DNA in cells so that their properties, or the chemicals which they produce, will be changed. Somatic cell therapy involves changes in some of the cells of the body of a person who has already been conceived. (*Soma* is the Greek word for "body.") These changes would not be passed on to that person's descendants. Germ line therapy, on the other hand, acts on sex cells or a fertilized ovum and intends to produce changes which will be inherited. Cloning a person means to take the nucleus of a cell of that person's body and insert it into a fertilized human ovum in place of the ovum's nucleus, and then getting the ovum to develop in the usual way to produce a baby with the same genetic makeup as the person from whose body the cell nucleus was taken.

Somatic cell therapy would be used to correct genetic errors which keep a person's body from producing necessary chemicals.[1] Men (and a few women — it's a sex-linked trait) with hemophilia, for example, do not produce a substance which is needed to make blood clot properly. It might be possible to change the cells which are supposed to produce this substance so that the person's blood would clot. Since this change would not affect the man's sperm cells, his descendants would still carry a gene for hemophilia.

Just as with the introduction of a new drug, such a therapy should be used only after extensive research and testing. But it does not seem to introduce any new theological or ethical issues beyond those already involved in the basic idea of medical intervention. Whether or not it's a good idea in individual cases might be argued, but there is no reason for fundamental opposition to somatic cell gene therapy. Such therapies have already been used on an experimental basis.

Things get more controversial when we come to germ line therapy and human cloning. The purpose of such technologies would be the development of human beings who are "designed" to have certain properties. Instead of simply changing the body of a person with hemophilia to correct that problem, we would be changing the basic genetic plan so that that person and his descendants would no longer have that genetic "defect."

The word "defect" was put in quotation marks in the last sentence because it's a term we need to be careful of. There is little problem with referring to hemophilia in that way because everybody recognizes that it's not a good thing to have. But we should reflect that the word "defective" usually refers to something produced by a factory: A tire or a piece of clothing may be defective, and if it is it will be thrown out or perhaps sold at a reduced price as something second-best. There is a danger in thinking of people in that way. We might be able to agree that it would be best to change the genetic structures which leads to certain kinds of mental retardation, but we should not consider people who have that trait as disposable.

Thus the idea that we should use genetic engineering to improve humanity calls for considerable caution. We may be able to agree that crippling genetic diseases should be eliminated, but other traits might not be so obvious. Some people, unfortunately, have the notion that certain skin colors represent "defects." If those people got to be in charge of a program for genetic improvement of the human race, what would the result be? That brings us back to a question asked by the Roman poet Juvenal long before genetic engineering was dreamed of : "Who will guard the guardians themselves?" How can we be sure that decisions really are made for the good of all?

We should also realize that improving humanity genetically is not as easy as it sounds. We might think of producing people with greater intelligence, or even with increased abilities for specialties such as mathematics or music. But there is no "music gene." Genes code for proteins, not directly for complex skills. Certainly heredity may have something to do with musical ability, as some of the sons of J. S. Bach suggest. But environment and the ways in which people are brought up and educated also have a good deal to do with it.

Could we get around those difficulties by avoiding the uncertainties involved with the offspring of a genius and cloning the genius directly? This might be done even with someone who has long been dead, if parts of the body or tissues were available. We could get a new Einstein or Mozart in this way.

Or could we? The clone of Einstein would be an infant, and would have to be brought up in some way in some environment, as all children are. Even differences of the environment of developing fetuses in the womb may have some significant effects. So we would get an identical twin of Albert who would probably have some of the same abilities, but there is no guarantee that he would be a world class physicist.

Cloning great men and women is rather remote from the concerns of most of us. What motives would there be for an ordinary person to have a clone of her/himself produced? Might it be as a replacement to console grieving parents who have lost a child? The comfort would be weak, at best. The idea that "I" would not cease to exist when my present body died as long as my clone still lived would be simply a delusion of immortality. Thus there are some serious questions about the good to be achieved by gene line therapy and human cloning.

To say that there are such questions is not the same as saying that use of these technologies would always be wrong. The very ideas of genetic engineering and cloning, as well as other bio-medical technologies, have sometimes been rejected because they would supposedly mean that we are "playing God." The claim that scientists are "playing God" may be taken as sufficient cause to condemn them.

People who use that phrase usually forget that there is a proper biblical sense in which humanity is *supposed* to "play God." God intended to "make humankind in our image, according to our likeness" (Genesis 1:26), and the psalmist tells us that "The heavens are the LORD's heavens, but the earth he has given to human beings" (Psalm 115:16). Human beings are, as we said in the previous chapter, supposed to be God's representatives in caring for the world. Problems arise when we want to act in the world as if we could depend only on our own powers and not have to be responsible to God.

There seems to be little doubt that human gene line therapy and cloning will eventually be done, for good or for ill. It isn't helpful either to reject these technologies entirely or simply to approve of them because they *can* be done. What we need to do is to consider appropriate guidelines for their use.

The most basic such guideline is that any human being produced as a result of these techniques must be treated as a fully human being, and be given the respect and protection which all people should have. They should in no way be second class citizens. This would mean, for example, that the notion of making clones of people and putting them in cold storage as a source of "spare parts" in case a heart or kidney is needed would definitely be ruled out. Living human beings are not to be mined for resources against their will.

With that last example we end our brief look at genetic technologies to consider another set of issues. Organ donation and transplants, once also considered to be only a subject for science fiction, are now standard medical practice. Donation and transplantation of tissue and organs goes back to the first successful blood transfusions and cornea transplants. In recent decades it has also become possible to transplant major organs such as the heart, lungs, liver, and kidneys. In large part this has been due to development of drugs which suppress the immune reactions of the recipient, so that the transplanted organ will not be rejected by the body. If a vital organ of a person is not functioning, it may be possible to replace it with one from a person who has just died. But while these procedures are now routinely successful for individuals, they are limited by the shortage of organs which are donated.

There are various reasons why people are reluctant to donate their own organs or those of relatives. Ignorance of the need and suspicion of the medical establishment are factors which can be dealt with by getting the word out about the good which can be done through organ donation and removing fears about experimentation and sale of organs. But some people also have religious objections to donating organs, and those objections can only be dealt with on religious grounds.

The primary religious concerns are related to ideas that the integrity of the body should not be violated because of belief in a future resurrection of the body. To put it simply, everyone will supposedly need his heart, kidneys, and so forth for the Last Day. And how can the same heart belong to two different people?

It isn't just transplants that raise this question. There is a continual recycling of molecules in nature, and some of those which belong to the body of one person today were part of another person's centuries ago. It's very likely that the next breath you take will contain oxygen atoms once breathed by King David! The sharing of material in this case is not as dramatic as with transplantation of entire organs, but it happens.

But if we look seriously at the concept of "the same material" in modern physics, this problem goes away. In quantum mechanics, identical particles really are identical and can't be distinguished from one another. We can say that we have two electrons or two carbon atoms in a system, but we can't label them individually and keep track of them. This means that the phrase "the same atom" has to be used with great caution. We can really speak only of two structures containing the same *pattern* of atoms of various types.

Saint Paul argues in 1 Corinthians 15:35-49 that the resurrection involves a transformation rather than a return to the same type of physical existence as before. We cannot describe the "spiritual body" of which Paul speaks simply in terms of our physics. But in whatever way the material of the present world may be taken up into it, we do not have to worry about how God will sort out "the same atoms" or "the same heart" that we had in earthly life.

107

Moreover, donating an organ is not just a neutral transfer of material from one body to another. It is an act of charity, a gift of life. If in the resurrection there were any signs of such donation, they would not be defects but marks of love, like the wounds of Christ (Luke 24:40, John 20:19-29).

Speaking of the resurrection may remind us of death. For no matter what medical breakthroughs there may be, death eventually has to be faced. Advances in medicine have paradoxically created problems here, often making dying more complicated and difficult than it used to be. Life support systems have made it possible to keep alive people with severe health problems far longer than in the past. In some cases this means that people are kept alive well past the point where there is any realistic chance for recovery or even consciousness. To what extent should these technologies be used, and at what point may it be right to turn off the machinery and let a person die?

Debate in this area is often marked by slogans — "Sanctity of life" versus "Quality of life." The first may be understood to mean that everything should be done to sustain physical life for as long as possible, while the second often implies that life should be ended, or allowed to end, when it is no longer a life of quality. This position is sometimes summarized as urging "death with dignity."

The first thing to realize is that the Bible does not give us a precise medical definition of just when life does end. Death is associated with the time when breathing stops (e.g., Psalm 104:29), for that, along with the stopping of the heart's beating, is an obvious indication of death in an age of relatively unsophisticated medicine. Today we can often restart heartbeat and breathing, and can sustain these activities even when a person is in a deep coma and would not be able to breathe spontaneously. We have machinery which will breathe for a person who is conscious but unable to breathe spontaneously. Brain death, the absence of electrical activity in the brain for a significant period, is now often used as the criterion for physical death, though this continues to be debated.

Having defined the time of death in medical terms, we are then left with the ethical questions. How long should death be postponed when illness is terminal, when it is clear that (barring a miracle) there is no possibility of recovery? Both "sanctity of life" and "quality of life" offer answers to this question. From a Christian standpoint, both answers are incomplete.

The significance of human life and death should be seen ultimately in light of the life and death of Jesus. And the death of Jesus was anything but dignified. Crucifixion was a form of execution which was painful, humiliating, and drawn out. It was deliberately used by the Roman state to terrify and intimidate the lower classes. Origen, a Christian theologian of the third century, summarized the way this form of execution was seen in the ancient world as "the most vile death of the cross."[2]

Of course we should do what is possible to relieve suffering. But if we believe in the saving power of the cross, we can't say that avoidance of suffering is the highest ethical good. In telling his disciples to take up their crosses and follow him (Mark 8:34-38), Jesus gives the whole life of the Christian this character. A life of genuine quality will not be a life free of suffering, even, in some cases, suffering which seems pointless to us.

We are going to die, and Christianity gives no promise that this reality will be changed as long as we are in the world. That is the meaning of the liturgy of Ash Wednesday in which each person is told, in words from Genesis 3:19, "Remember that you are dust, and to dust you shall return." The story of Jesus, though, does not end with death but with resurrection. That means that the hope which the Christian message offers is not one to be achieved by staving off death for every possible hour. It is the hope of resurrection, of new life in spite of the reality of death. Insisting upon "sanctity of life" may focus so strongly on sustaining life that it misses the hope of the resurrection.

So what is the answer? These considerations do not give us a neat answer in the form of an exact definition of when a life support apparatus ought to be turned off. They are, instead, general principles which Christians ought to bring to difficult decisions which have to be made about life and death.

In making *any* ethical decision, whether about the use of biomedical technology or in some other area, it's essential for Christians to remember that they are not finally saved by always making the right choices. We should try to make important decisions as prayerfully and as thoughtfully as possible, consulting with people who have expertise when necessary. But we will sometimes come to the point where we have to make a decision and we're not 100 percent sure what the best decision is. The fact that we are justified by grace for Christ's sake means that we can dare to make the decision without total ethical certainty. We can do this in the confidence that we are justified, that we are God's people, even if we make the wrong choice. God who "justifies the ungodly" (Romans 4:5) certainly justifies those who try but fail to do the right thing!

Topics For Discussion

1. In 2 Chronicles 16:12, King Asa seems to be criticized for seeking help from physicians. Why? (It may help to read the preceding verses 7-11.)

2. A distinction is made in the Roman Catholic tradition between "natural" methods of birth control, which are allowed, and "artificial" methods, which are forbidden. Is this is a helpful distinction? Why or why not?

3. You can live a healthy life with just one good kidney. Should a person be allowed to sell one of his or her kidneys to the highest bidder?

4. Couples will sometimes go to great lengths to have children who are their biological descendants (or perhaps descendants of only one of them) by procedures such as *in vitro* fertilization or surrogate motherhood instead of adopting children. Why? To what extent should technology be used to enable such desires to be carried out?

1. Genetic engineering can also be used to produce proteins in biological cultures outside the human body. This is now done for human growth hormone and insulin, for example.

2. Martin Hengel, *Crucifixion* (Fortress, Philadelphia, 1977), p. xi.

Chapter 12

Angels, Aliens, And AI

The relationship between God and humanity has had a central place in our discussions so far. We recognized that we are not separated from the rest of creation. Biological evolution means that we are related to other species, extinct and alive, and ecology shows that our welfare is linked with what happens to nature. But it is natural for us to concentrate on our own place in the scheme of things.

We should, however, consider the possibility that we are not the only intelligent beings in the universe. What can science tell us about that possibility? And if there are other rational creatures, how do they fit into the theological picture? How should we act toward them? In this chapter we'll take a quick look at those issues.

What other rational creatures might exist? There are three basic categories that we might consider. First, the Christian tradition (as well as Judaism and Islam) has talked about the existence of *angels*, good and bad. Second, as a great deal of science fiction and some serious science often remind us, intelligent life may have evolved in places in the universe beyond the earth. There may be extraterrestrial *aliens* — sometimes abbreviated ETs. And finally, work with computers might bring into being *artificial intelligence* — or AI for short. Let's consider these possibilities in turn.

The word "angel" means "messenger," and in the Bible the angels are sometimes connected with "the heavenly host." We see both of these aspects in the familiar Christmas story in Luke 2:1-20. "The host of heaven" can also refer to the stars. The Bible gives us very little detail about angels, good or bad. If they are supernatural beings, at some level of reality beyond our physical universe, then there is little that science could say about them. Speaking about them may serve to keep science humble, to remind us of the scope of God's creation and that we can't learn everything there is to know about it.

In some places the New Testament sees angelic beings, like the "rulers of this age" in 1 Corinthians 2:6-8 or the "elemental spirits" of Galatians 4:1-11, as cosmic forces which stand behind and empower the political and religious structures of the world. From a modern standpoint, this is a "mythical" idea which biblical writers used to speak of the way in which Christ accomplishes God's purpose of liberation. But to say that this language is "mythical" doesn't mean that we should ignore it. We may look for things in our own situation which correspond to it. The fact that the basic energies of the universe, such as nuclear weapons and other technologies, empower political and economic structures in our world is significant and suggests that these might have roles corresponding to the cosmic forces of the New Testament.

The early Christians saw the Roman state as part of God's ordering of the world, as in Romans 13:1-7, but in the book of Revelation it is pictured as demonic because it claims divine honors. In the same way, science and technology and the political and economic systems which they support are not evil, but become so when we allow ourselves to place our ultimate trust in them. Again, we are reminded that science and technology are not our highest goods.

Both science fiction and science itself have given a great deal more attention to the possibility of extraterrestrial intelligence. This is not a new idea: Scientists as far back as the seventeenth century speculated about a "plurality of worlds" and what the inhabitants of other planets of the solar system might be like. We are now quite certain that there is no intelligent life, and perhaps no life at any level, anywhere in the solar system besides the earth — though the possibility that microscopic life forms might have existed on Mars billions of years ago remains open. But we also know that there are billions of other stars similar to our own just in our galaxy, and the fact that life evolved on earth suggests that it might well have evolved at other sites in the universe as well.

That sounds reasonable, but it's quite difficult to make anything like a reliable estimate of encountering another intelligent species. There are about a hundred billion stars in our galaxy, and we now know that many of the nearer ones have planets orbiting them. While those planets are much larger than earth, there probably are also smaller worlds which we have not detected. So it seems likely that there are millions of planets at least roughly similar to the earth in size and composition.

But now we run into a problem, because we don't have any idea of the probability of the chemical evolution of life in an environment like that of the primitive earth. We only have one example — our own world — in which that has happened, and we don't actually know the physical and chemical processes which enabled it to happen. We don't know if what happened on earth was extremely common or tremendously against the odds. There is no point in saying, "Well, then, let's make a conservative estimate of the probability of life developing," because, with our lack of information, we don't even know whether an estimate is pessimistic or optimistic. And once life does develop, we again don't know the probability of an intelligent species like our own evolving. This only happened once on earth, as far as we know, and we don't know the details by which it took place.

There is one argument, based on the anthropic principles which we discussed in Chapter 9, that intelligent life is *not* plentiful in the universe. As we saw there, the universe would apparently have to be as old as it is, and thus as big as it is, for intelligent life to have evolved. If the universe is just old enough and big enough for this to have happened, the argument goes, then it is fairly likely that it has only happened once. This argument can be strengthened by asking the question, "Where are they?" That is, if there *are* other intelligent species, and especially if they developed significantly earlier than we did, why haven't we had any communication from them? (And in spite of all the attention given to UFO enthusiasts, there is no solid evidence that other species have visited earth, either in the distant past or today.)

The argument based on the Anthropic Principle is only statistical, and wouldn't rule out the existence of intelligent life on a handful of other planets. And there might be reasons why an advanced species would deliberately avoid contact with ours. Our galaxy is probably not just teeming with life, but we don't have to conclude that we're utterly alone in it.

If intelligent life does exist elsewhere, it's likely that our contact with it will be by means of electromagnetic signals, radio, and television. Einstein's relativity and the energy sources we have available put limits on the time it would take for us to reach other solar systems. We don't know today how to accelerate a spaceship to even half the speed of light, and even if we could, it would take decades to reach the nearest stars. Perhaps there are radical breakthroughs in basic theory and technology which will make possible some type of "warp drive," but they haven't been made yet. For the foreseeable future we'll have to be content with radio communication and the long delays in any such conversation imposed by the finite speed of transmission.

Let's suppose for the sake of argument that other intelligent species have come into being somewhere in the universe, and that we have unmistakable contact with them. How would we evaluate these facts theologically?

The Bible tells us nothing at all, pro or con, about life on other planets. There is no reason to think that God couldn't have created life on other worlds through the same types of evolutionary processes which took place on earth. Since our own evolution embodies the results of many accidents of evolutionary history (such as the asteroid impact which destroyed the dinosaurs), another intelligent species should be expected to be very different from ours in physical makeup, modes of thought, and so forth. We can probably assume that its basic chemistry would be based on carbon and that water would be important for it because we don't know of any other possibilities. But beyond that, there is no reason to think that another rational species would have to have two legs and eyes, be bisexual, or have any of the other features which we associate with *Homo sapiens*.

The existence of extraterrestrial life would pose no problems for the doctrine of creation. Where questions arise is in relation to the concept of salvation. The New Testament indicates that Jesus Christ is the one in whom God reconciles and saves not only humanity but "all things," as in Colossians 1:20. Of course, as we noted, the Bible doesn't address the question of species on other planets, so one could argue that the biblical writers simply didn't take them into account. Perhaps so. On the other hand, the strong language of Colossians about "all things, whether on earth or in heaven," certainly makes it sound as if the writer meant everything, whatever it might be.

One possibility is that other intelligent species have not sinned as our species has, and thus are not in need of redemption. The arguments which we made in connection with human evolution, suggesting that it would have been hard for early humans to *avoid* sin, make this debatable, though it is a possibility. But what if other species have sinned? How could Jesus of Nazareth be their savior?

The traditional Christian position is that salvation has come through the Incarnation: Our humanity is saved because the Second Person of the Trinity became fully human. This can be seen as a restatement of Hebrews 2:17, "He had to become like his brothers and sisters in every respect."[1] We pointed out in Chapter 8 that our own humanity includes the evolutionary history which we have in common with other terrestrial species, so that in some sense they are "included" in Christ's humanity. But how could Christ be the savior of extraterrestrials?

One way of thinking about this is to relate salvation to the pre-incarnate Christ, an "unfleshed Word." Such a proposal is unsatisfactory to those who emphasize the importance of the Word *made flesh*. The passage from Colossians 1 does, after all, speak about the reconciliation of "all things ... through the blood of his cross." But there is some support in the Christian tradition for the idea that all truly rational beings participate in the Word of God. In the second century the Christian teacher Justin Martyr wrote:

> *We have been taught that Christ is the first-born of God, and we have declared above that He is the Word of whom every race of men were partakers; and those who lived reasonably [literally "with reason" or "with the Word"] are Christians, even though they have been thought atheists....*[2]

Another possibility is to speak of the Incarnation as a cosmic event in a realistic sense. Martin Luther, for example, argued that the divine property of omnipresence, being everywhere, is communicated to the human nature of Jesus. In passages which speak of Christ being "seated at the right hand of the Father," Luther understood God's "right hand" to mean divine power and authority and said "the right hand of God is everywhere." This idea of the humanity of Christ being present to the entire universe no doubt seems strange at first glance. However, quantum mechanical ideas about "nonlocality" may be helpful here. Particles which have once interacted remain in a way "entangled" with one another, and this may provide some way of making scientific (as distinguished from theological) sense of Luther's idea.

Finally, we may simply think of the way in which Christ normally comes to people on earth — through the proclamation of the gospel. In the proclamation of Christ, Christ is made present. (It is, of course, no accident that Christ is called "the Word" in the Gospel of John.) This might call the church to a mission of proclamation of the gospel to any extraterrestrials we might encounter. Of course such a mission should renounce the exploitation and colonialism which all too often have accompanied Christian missionaries on earth.

The letter to the Ephesians tells us that it is part of God's plan "that through the church the wisdom of God in its rich variety might now be made known to the rulers and authorities in the heavenly places" (Ephesians 3:10). That referred originally to the idea of angelic powers and the fact that they too (according to Ephesians 1:10) are to find their fulfillment in Christ. But it may not stretch the sense too much if we think of this verse as a calling to a mission which is extraterrestrial in the sense in which we use the word today.

The third category of rational creatures which we might encounter is *artificial intelligence*. Here there is not simply doubt about whether such things *do* exist, but debate about whether or not they *could* exist.

There has been a tremendous increase in what electronic computers can do since their beginnings in the 1940s. They are able to store huge amounts of data and do calculations far faster than any human being. It would be difficult to imagine our modern technological society without computers. A good deal has also been accomplished in robotics, so that a computer need no longer be fixed in place. It can move around and perform physical operations. But could a computer actually become conscious and think in the same ways that we are able to think?

Computers operate according to systems of mathematical facts and operations, like those used in arithmetic with ordinary numbers. And one of the surprising things which came to the attention of mathematicians in the twentieth century is that such mathematical systems have built in limitations. There will be reasonable questions which can be asked of the system, but which cannot be given a "yes" or "no" answer within the system. There are, as mathematicians say, "undecidable propositions." We may be able to "intuit" an answer to the question, but that answer can't be reached just by following the formal mathematical rules.

If computers then operate according to the rules of such a system, can they overcome its limitations? Can they do the same kinds of things that human brains can do? Or to put the question the other way around, are our brains simply "computers made out of meat" instead of from metals and semiconductors and plastics? The human brain, after all, evolved through natural processes, and at some historical period, in some way, our ability to think emerged from those processes. Perhaps artificial intelligence would emerge in a similar way if a computer became sufficiently complex. Those who believe that artificial intelligence is possible think that the work with computers might parallel human evolution, but the issue isn't really settled.

How would we test a claim for artificial intelligence? We could make use of a test proposed by the British mathematician Alan Turing. In essence, we would let the claimant to artificial intelligence answer any arbitrary set of questions. The candidate would be concealed from us and we would get responses in the form of answers printed on a tape or by some other means which would not prejudice us by appearance, sound of voice, or any other incidental features. In other words, we wouldn't know whether a computer or a human being was sitting behind the screen. And if the computer could answer all our questions in such a way that we would be unable to distinguish it from a human being, we would have to say that it was intelligent in the same way that we are.

We needn't enter further here into the question of the logical possibility of artificial intelligence. But we should ask about its *theo*logical possibility and the religious implications if it does come into being.

Some Christians have felt that the possibility of artificial intelligence should be rejected on religious grounds, but there doesn't seem to be a very strong argument for that position. Even if an intelligent computer is brought into being by our science and technology, we would see God at work through that human activity just as we see God at work in all the things which go on in the world. The fact that we refer to *artificial* intelligence, meaning that it is a work of human technology, would not make it any less something which God has made possible.

Whether or not such a computer would have a soul, or be a moral agent, is another matter. Those are theological and ethical questions, and the fact that a computer could pass the Turing test would not automatically answer them. It may be that a breakthrough to reflective consciousness, such as happened in human evolution, is enough to make something a morally responsible being. Even if becoming such a being requires that God in some way miraculously "insert" a soul into it (which is the traditional Roman Catholic view), we have no grounds for asserting that God would *not* put a soul into a sufficiently developed computer. Nor can we insist that God *would* do this.

Perhaps we simply have to wait and see if artificial intelligence is developed to get answers to those questions. The prospect of carrying out a meaningful theological conversation with a robot is challenging. Ethical questions would also be raised by such a development. If artificial intelligence is accompanied by moral responsibility, we will not be able to do just anything we please with it. Would shutting down such a computer be a personal assault on it? Some thought needs to be given to such questions before the prospect becomes a reality.

Topics For Discussion

1. Many people who have little interest in science in general are fascinated by the ideas of UFOs and contacts with aliens. Why?

2. We talked here about angels and extraterrestrials as if they were two different things. Is it possible that some of the biblical accounts of angels are about extraterrestrials?

3. If human beings do someday create computers with genuine intelligence, will we have any moral obligations to them?

---

1. The NRSV version quoted here uses inclusive language. A more literal translation of the Greek is "He had to be made like his brethren in every respect" (RSV). But here inclusive language is needed to bring out the correct sense. If God had assumed some human nature which excluded women, then women could not be saved through the Incarnation.

2. "The First Apology of Justin" in *The Ante-Nicene Fathers*, Volume 1 (Eerdmans, Grand Rapids, Michigan, 1979), p. 178.

Chapter 13

Religious Themes In Science Fiction

Until quite recently two of the possible "others" which we have just discussed, extraterrestrials and artificial intelligence, were more likely to be encountered in science fiction than in serious scientific work. (Angels, on the other hand, would be more likely to be subjects for fantasy literature — though the boundary between science fiction and fantasy is not sharp.) As we saw in the previous chapter, it is still unclear whether the aliens and intelligent robots of science fiction will ever become a reality. But science fiction does not, in any case, simply try to predict scientific developments. Sometimes it has done that successfully, and in other cases it has missed the mark. (While hundreds of stories were written before 1969 about a first landing on the moon, no one guessed that the whole world would watch the first human step on the moon via live television.) Good science fiction explores *possible* futures and possible worlds and, by doing that, gives us some insight into the human condition and perhaps into broader realities. All that, of course, is in addition simply to being entertaining, which is not a negligible matter.

We want to discuss here some ways in which science fiction has dealt with themes which have a religious dimension. Science fiction doesn't appeal to everyone, and readers who simply aren't interested in it may want to skim this chapter lightly or skip it. But since much of the popular understanding of science is influenced, for good or for bad, by science fiction, it does seem worthwhile to spend a little time on the subject.

Religion is an important feature of the human condition, so possible futures will have a religious dimension. It's true that in some popular science fiction, any human religious belief or practice is simply ignored. That is the case, for example, in the *Star Trek* series and movies. Humanity in this vision of the future seems

123

to have almost no religious beliefs or practices. This is a striking contrast to aliens like the Klingons or Bajorans, for whom religion is an integral part of their culture. This peculiarity can be traced largely to the anti-religious attitudes of *Star Trek* creator Gene Roddenberry[1] rather than to anything about science fiction itself. (And it is perhaps significant that the Klingon and Bajoran cultures in *Star Trek* are simply more *interesting* than the rather bland human one, which seems to have no purpose other than "to go where no one has gone before.") Another television series, *Babylon 5*, treated both human and alien religions with some respect.

Visions of the future can be misleading because it's a temptation for a writer to make the future look like what he or she thinks it *should* be, or would *like* it to be. An atheist can film a story which "shows" that religion will disappear as people become more enlightened, and a Christian can make one which "proves" that the Second Coming will happen soon. Both are fiction. Either one could be worth seeing if it honestly tried to explore the significance of that future, or a waste of time if it just tried to bully the viewer into agreeing with the writer.

This shouldn't be taken to mean that science fiction has no religious interest unless it has characters praying or preaching or discussing theology. Religion has been spoken of as involving matters of "ultimate concern," and anything which explores the most fundamental questions of life will be of religious interest, even if religion is not an explicit theme of the work.

A good example of this is the 1956 film *Forbidden Planet*. A spaceship from earth arrives at the planet Altair 4 in search of survivors from an expedition sent out twenty years earlier. They find only one survivor, Dr. Morbius, with his daughter and a robot which he has constructed. All the others, Morbius tells them, were "torn limb from limb" by some unseen force. Morbius has spent the intervening time studying the remains of the Krell, an advanced civilization which inhabited the planet 200,000 years before. The Krell had developed a tremendous planet-wide system of machinery which was to culminate all their efforts, but were somehow destroyed in their hour of greatest achievement. As soon as the spacecraft lands, its crew members start to be attacked, one by one, by the same invisible force which had devastated the earlier expedition.

The Krell machinery is found to have been a device to give form to their thoughts and desires, to give them anything they wished by pure mentality. But they had failed to reckon with the "mindless primitive" which remained as part of their brains from earlier stages of evolution. It is these "monsters from the Id" which had destroyed the Krell in a single night. And the same type of monsters from the depths of Morbius' mind destroyed his fellow humans when his peaceful existence on Altair 4 was threatened.

Forbidden Planet makes no reference to the Christian tradition, but a little reflection will connect it with our discussion of evolution and sin in Chapter 8. As we pointed out there, the first humans would have inherited a considerable load of behaviors which would not have been "sin" in our pre-human ancestors (to whom the term sin doesn't apply) but would be sinful for morally responsible creatures. This raises some questions about how it might be possible to understand the Christian teaching that humanity was created with "original righteousness" which it lost because of a deliberate choice of sin. The movie does not answer the theological questions involved with this topic, but it can provoke some serious thought about them.

Charles L. Harness' novel *The Paradox Men* (Crown, New York, 1984) gets at the same issues in a different way. In the setting of a run-up to final nuclear war between world empires in the twenty-second century, the mysterious Alar, a man with superhuman powers, is pursued across the solar system. He defeats his enemies but plunges to his death in the sun, and hurtles backward in time, as the nuclear exchange begins. Alar goes back some 40,000 years to change not only history but human nature itself, to alter fundamentally the aggressive and destructive course of our species.

Isaac Asimov was one of the most prolific writers of science fiction and produced dozens of books on all kinds of other topics as well. With a doctorate in chemistry, he brought more scientific expertise to his craft than many writers do. Asimov was an atheist, but his novels seldom show any hostility toward religion (though they usually ignore it), and some of his short stories make use of religious ideas in semi-serious ways. One of his more interesting contributions, however, touches on the ethical issues connected with artificial intelligence to which we referred at the end of the last chapter.

In his stories about robots, Asimov used three "laws of robotics" which limit robotic action toward human beings: In essence, these laws state that robots cannot injure humans, that they must obey humans, and that they must protect their own existence — in that order of priority. These are rules which human beings might very well build into robots, but it is significant that they only limit robotic action toward humans. Human beings have no moral obligations toward robots, who may turn off their machines when it's convenient to do so. This means that humanity has created a very sophisticated slave class, an idea which the very word "robot" expresses: It was first used in a 1920 play by the Czech writer Karel Capek, and means "worker." But science fiction, including some of Asimov's stories, also has explored the possibility of robots going beyond the limits set by the laws of robotics, and perhaps becoming the destroyers, or the saviors, or the successors, of humanity.

Since science fiction often (though not always) deals with the future, the question of what humanity will be in the future is sometimes part of the story. This can be done either in terms of possibilities for human evolution or visions of alien species which differ in important ways from humanity. It is interesting that human evolution, when it is a plot device, usually takes the form of the development of super *individuals* with new mental powers — enhanced intelligence, telepathy, and so forth. On the other hand, any sort of *collective* development is usually pictured as malevolent. The Borg of *Star Trek: Next Generation* are an excellent example. With their huge cubic spaceships and the mechanized corpse-like appearance of the collective's units, they seem the embodiment of a pitiless force bent on wiping out whatever is genuinely human when they announce, "Resistance is futile. Prepare to be assimilated."

The Borg and other collectives of science fiction (and especially American science fiction) show the distrust of termite colony futures toward which the totalitarian movements of the twentieth century seemed to be pushing humanity. There is a legitimate concern about individuality being crushed out. But an excessive concern for individuality may also miss a major aspect of evolution which was emphasized by Pierre Teilhard de Chardin.

Teilhard was a paleontologist and Jesuit priest whose life work was devoted to understanding evolution in a Christian way. He pointed out that evolution had involved things *coming together* — complex chemicals to form living cells and single cells into multicellular organisms. He argued that the formation of societies of individual organisms, and specifically the formation of human societies, was part of this process. The next stage of evolution, he believed, would be the coming together of human beings into a super-personal organism. He came to that idea not just from scientific study but also from theological reflection. For in a number of places the New Testament uses the image of the *body of Christ* to speak of the church.

First Corinthians 12:12-31 is an especially important presentation of this idea. Paul says, "Now you are the body of Christ and individually members of it" (v. 27). And his whole argument here is that being part of the body doesn't mean that all members are the same. Just as different parts of a human body have different functions, and so can each be good at what they do for the good of all, "so it is with Christ" (v. 12). In other words, understanding the unity as an organic body rather than just a homogeneous mass gives a picture very different from that of the fearsome "collective."

It would be interesting to see this idea developed in a science fiction story. That would probably require some explicit exploration of Christian ideas. And in fact, some good science fiction has openly utilized religious ideas and themes.

Thoughtful uses of such themes can provide challenges for believers. James Blish's disturbing novel *A Case of Conscience* (Ballantine, 1958) confronts us with the ancient Manichaean heresy, which is basically the idea that the devil has creative power on the same level as God's. In Arthur C. Clarke's short story "The Star" (in *The Other Side of the Sky* [Harcourt, Brace, & World, 1958]), a Jesuit astrophysicist on an expedition to another solar system has to deal with the discovery that the explosion of the star which destroyed a magnificent civilization was the Star of

Bethlehem! That might be taken simply as a put-down of Christianity. (Clarke, who is best known to the general public for the film *2001: a space odyssey*, is not very friendly to religion.) But it can also challenge us to think about a concept that Martin Luther spoke of: God does work which is "alien" to the divine nature in order to accomplish his "proper" work.

Futuristic fiction can also remind us about the dangers of religion, such as its use to achieve and hold political power. "If This Goes On — ," one of the stories in Robert A. Heinlein's "future history series," is set in a United States under the dictatorship of "the Prophet." (Most of Heinlein's future history stories are collected in *The Past Through Tomorrow* [G.P. Putnam's Sons, 1967].)

A more positive view of a future Christianity is central to Walter M. Miller, Jr.'s *A Canticle for Leibowitz* (Bantam, New York, 1959). Here the remnants of civilization are again saved by monks in the new Dark Age after the nuclear "flame deluge." The novels and short stories of Philip K. Dick, such as *The Divine Invasion* (Simon and Schuster, 1981), often make use of parts of the Jewish and Christian traditions. While his ideas are usually far from orthodox, they are challenging — when the reader can follow Dick's sometimes confusing plot twists.

The "space trilogy" of C. S. Lewis, *Out of the Silent Planet*, *Perelandra*, and *That Hideous Strength* (all in Macmillan paperbacks), was an attempt by a Christian writer to present an alternative to what he saw as the anti-Christian tendency of a good deal of British science fiction of the early twentieth century. The physical descriptions of the planets in these novels are outdated — we know now that liquid water, let alone life, could not exist on the surface of Venus. But the form which Lewis gave to the Christian concepts of fall and redemption, and his warnings about the dangers of science and technology loosed from moral foundations, are still worth reading.

Science fiction writers may also make use of religious themes outside the Judaeo-Christian tradition. The rather vague spirituality of the *Star Wars* films, centered on "The Force," could be understood in a Christian sense, but is more aligned with religious traditions of the East. Some people in the scientific community got upset when Luke Skywalker, in the first movie of the series, turns off his targeting computer to let himself be guided by The Force in the climactic attack on the Death Star. But perhaps technology *can't* solve all problems.

Even when it doesn't deal with any themes of religious significance, good science fiction can be helpful just because it gets us used to thinking about possibilities and change. Science fiction can stretch our thinking in a number of ways. And at this point we need to have our thinking stretched because we are going on to discuss the future of the human race and the future of the universe — not simply in fictional terms but (as much as we are able) real ones.

Topics For Discussion

1. Science fiction films which could be viewed and discussed profitably by a group include *Alien, Blade Runner, Contact, Deep Impact, E.T.: The Extra-Terrestrial, Forbidden Planet, Star Wars, The Matrix,* and *2001: A Space Odyssey.* Most do not have obviously "religious" themes, but they all raise issues of some religious significance.

2. What would a "Christian" version of a television series like *Star Trek* be like?

3. The concept of "parallel worlds" has been popular among science fiction writers. Philip K. Dick's *The Man in the High Castle* (Vintage, 1991), for example, is set in a United States in which Germany and Japan won World War II. Are there any interesting ways in which this plot device could be used with religious themes?

---

1. Joel Engel, *Gene Roddenberry: The Myth and the Man behind Star Trek* (Hyperion, New York, 1994), especially pp. 246-247.

Chapter 14

The Future

Christianity has always been to a greater or lesser extent oriented toward the future. As we saw in our discussion of Genesis, even at the beginning of the Bible the image of the Sabbath points forward, toward the fulfillment of God's plan for creation.

The prophets of Israel gave their people promises of a future in which God's kingdom would be established in its fullness and in which the true king, the Messiah, would reign. In some of the last parts of the Old Testament to be written (Isaiah 26:19, Daniel 12:1-3) there is the hope of a resurrection of the dead associated with this future. Thus the hope of many Jews in the time of Jesus, like Martha of Bethany, was that the dead "will rise again in the resurrection on the last day" (John 11:24).

We should pause here to reflect a bit on this idea of resurrection because it is sometimes seen as an idea which has to be eliminated or understood in some figurative way in a scientific age. But one doesn't need modern science to have doubts about resurrection. Some of the philosophically-inclined crowd at Athens "scoffed" when Paul spoke of "the resurrection of the dead" (Acts 17:32). Modern science actually helps to get rid of some old objections to this doctrine. We saw in Chapter 11 that the question of having "the same material" in two resurrected bodies becomes a non-problem in quantum theory. Frank Tipler, whose extreme version of the Anthropic Principle we noted in Chapter 9, has argued that it would be possible for a sufficiently powerful computer to run a perfect simulation of a human being with all relevant memories and experiences, and that this program would be indistinguishable, both from within and without, from the original person.

Those are interesting speculations, but they don't really get at the heart of the biblical concept of resurrection. Its point is not simply return to the same kind of life as before, the sort of revival which the Bible describes in the story of Jairus' daughter (Mark

5:35-43). She eventually had to die, but "Christ, being raised from the dead, will never die again; death no longer has dominion over him" (Romans 6:9). Resurrection means a new *kind* of life, a life which is perfectly in touch with God and attuned to God's will. That is why Paul says, in speaking of the resurrection, "It is sown a physical body, it is raised a spiritual body" (1 Corinthians 15:44). There is continuity between the physical and spiritual body, like that between a seed and a full grown plant, but this continuity does not mean that the body which is to be raised will be simply the body which died. "This perishable body must put on imperishability," Paul says, "and this mortal body must put on immortality" (1 Corinthians 15:53).

But we are getting ahead of the story. For the Christian view of resurrection and the last things is not based on some general philosophy about the future. It depends fundamentally on what happened to Jesus of Nazareth.

Even though the hopes of Jesus' disciples were dashed by his humiliating death on the cross, his resurrection brought them to believe that he was indeed God's Messiah. It was natural then to expect that his promise to come again would be fulfilled very soon, and that the Kingdom of God in its fullness would be ushered in. The early Christians eagerly awaited this coming again of Christ "on the clouds of heaven" (Matthew 24:30).[1] But time passed, and this didn't take place. We see the disturbance this caused in the Christian community in what is perhaps the latest writing of the New Testament, 2 Peter. In its third chapter this addresses the challenge of "scoffers" who say, "Where is the promise of his coming? For ever since our ancestors died, all things continue as they were from the beginning of creation!" (2 Peter 3:4). Theologians sometimes refer to this problem of the early church as "the delay of the *parousia*," using the Greek word which is translated as "coming" in the above passage.

In the light of modern cosmology, we can perhaps see things a little differently. Nearly 2,000 years have passed since the first Easter and the end of the world hasn't happened. On the scale of recorded human history, two millennia is quite a long time. But in proportion to ten billion or more years that have passed since the big bang it is negligible. On a cosmic scale there has really been no delay of the parousia at all!

But more is involved here than just the matter of time scale. Our usual way of speaking about "the End" is, of course, that it is something still to come. The resurrection is still ahead of us. But the resurrection of Jesus has happened as something in (though not limited to) history, in approximately A.D. 30. That means that in some way God's final future has broken into history. "If Jesus has been raised," theologian Wolfhart Pannenberg says, "then the end of the world has begun."[2] In other words, what we are told about God's future is summed up in the Easter message, "Jesus is risen."

That message is not first of all about resurrection in general. Nor is it simply "Someone is risen." The claim that Jesus of Nazareth has been raised beyond death is a claim that the kind of person Jesus is, his life and death, show us what the future is. That means that it is a life of total commitment to God the Father, a life of openness to others, of healing and forgiveness, of acceptance of suffering and death. That is why Easter is good news. A proclamation that the evil emperor Nero had been raised from the dead would be *bad* news because it would mean that the kind of life which Nero represented was the ultimate future of the world.

If Jesus' resurrection is the presence of the future, then the life of the Christian community will involve participation in God's future. Christians are spoken of in the letter to the Hebrews as having "tasted the goodness of the word of God and the powers of the age to come" (Hebrews 6:5). For all the value which tradition and memory of the past have, Christianity is oriented not to the past but to the future — even when it looks "back" to Easter.

The statement that Jesus will "come again" is often pictured in terms of his coming into the world from some realm beyond it. But this ignores another aspect of the gospel, Jesus' promise that "I am with you always, to the end of the age" (Matthew 28:20). While he is not visibly present as he was 2,000 years ago, he is present, and in one sense his "coming again" will be a manifestation of his presence now in the universe.

In fact, one way of reading the whole biblical story is as an account of God's preparation of the universe as a temple and dwelling. God's presence with the people of Israel was not initially connected with any fixed "holy place" but with a tent shrine which travelled with them on their journey through the wilderness. David's proposal to build a temple for God was met with some coolness by the prophet Nathan in 2 Samuel 7:1-17. There was always some tension between the idea of a dwelling of God in Jerusalem and God's own "Do I not fill heaven and earth?" (Jeremiah 23:24). In the Gospel of John, Jesus' words in 2:19-21 mean that he himself takes the place of the Temple. The Greek word translated "live" in "The Word became flesh and lived among us" (John 1:14) could be rendered literally as "dwell in a tent." It harks back to God's presence with Israel in the wilderness, and means that in Jesus God is present with us on our cosmic journey. At the end of that journey, in the highly symbolic language of Revelation, "the holy city, the new Jerusalem" (Revelation 21:2) comes down from heaven to the renewed earth, and "its temple is the Lord God the Almighty and the Lamb" (Revelation 21:22).

That is where the anthropic principles which we discussed in Chapter 9 seem to have their greatest theological significance. The anthropic "coincidences" allow intelligent life to evolve, but that is not an end in itself. God's purpose, as Ephesians 1:10 indicates, is the Incarnation, intelligent life indwelt by God. Through that indwelling, God will bring "all things" into communion with the divine life.

There is no biblical guarantee that God's future will arrive painlessly and bring the faithful all they dream of. Scripture has many images of destruction associated with the end times. The "day of God" will be a day in which "the heavens will be set ablaze and dissolved, and the elements will melt with fire" (2 Peter 3:12). But that same passage goes on immediately to speak of "new heavens and a new earth" (2 Peter 3:13 — see also Isaiah 65:17 and 66:22 and Revelation 21:1). God's future is not directed simply toward destruction of the universe or escape from it. Instead, creation is to be renewed. The ultimate future is not "going to heaven": In Revelation, the souls in heaven are refugees from the persecution and disasters happening on earth, waiting for the new heaven and earth. When that happens the heavenly city comes to earth, and "people will bring into it the glory and the honor of the nations" (Revelation 21:26). Everything good which has been accomplished in the course of human history is part of that final future.

Scientifically, there is a great deal that we don't know about the future. Science deals spectacularly well with general laws, but the prediction of the outcome of a specific set of events may be a very touchy matter. Chaos theory has revealed the phenomenon of "sensitivity to initial conditions," the fact that small changes in starting data too small for us to take into account may make radical changes in our predictions of outcomes. We would, for example, like to be able to predict the course of biological evolution, but an unexpected comet or asteroid could change all expectations, as it did for the dinosaurs some sixty-seven million years ago.

We can make some very general guesses about the course of human evolution. It seems likely that we will be able to affect our *cultural* evolution more and more through education, and we may be able to direct our *physical* and *behavioral* evolution to some extent through genetic engineering. It is possible that work with computers and artificial intelligence will lead to closer and closer links between human minds and computers, so that our biological evolution and our technological developments will become intertwined. But suggestions that we will eventually be *succeeded* in evolution by machine intelligence seem highly speculative at the present time.

In the previous chapter we called attention to Teilhard de Chardin's suggestion that human society itself is evolving into a super-personal organism. This was both a scientific and a theological proposal: Teilhard thought that humanity sixty years ago was being forced together toward this development, and that it would be connected with the development of the Body of Christ. Since then we have seen worldwide cooperation in some areas, and the Internet and other communications technologies have brought the people of the world together in ways that people never imagined in the early twentieth century. But the years since the end of the Cold War have also seen a resurgence of nationalism, ethnic hatreds, and divisive religious fundamentalisms which seem to be working against the type of evolution which Teilhard had in mind. The process of the human race coming together seems to be one of fits and starts, accompanied by a good deal of fragmentation. If this is the next stage in evolution, it appears to be moving slowly. But bearing in mind what we said earlier about the cosmological time scale, we should perhaps not be too surprised about that.

In purely scientific terms, we ultimately should think in terms of that cosmological time scale. Einstein's theory of gravitation allows an infinite number of models of the universe, but there are two basic possibilities which need to be considered. We have already looked briefly at them in Chapter 7. One possibility is that there is enough matter in the universe for its gravitation to cause cosmic expansion eventually to reverse itself. This is the space of positive curvature. In this case there would eventually be a "big crunch," a reverse of the big bang at the beginning. The other possibility (which includes the spaces of zero and negative curvature) is that the cosmic expansion continues forever. At the time of writing, this latter type of model seems to be most consistent with astronomical observations. In fact, the expansion even seems to be speeding up. However, scientific opinion about these matters has fluctuated over the past few decades and we are not yet able to make a statement about which model is best with complete confidence.

The model with a big crunch has temperatures which increase without bound as the ultimate collapse is approached. On the other hand, the models in which expansion never ceases have temperatures which drop closer and closer toward absolute zero. It is difficult to see how any kind of life that we know of could survive such conditions. But it is possible in principle in some models of both types for an infinite amount of new *information* to be processed. *If* artificial intelligence is possible, and if computers can be built at the level of the most elementary particles, then it might be possible for such artificial intelligence in a sense to have an infinite amount of *experience*.

The fact that our present scientific understanding enables us to sketch some possible features of God's future is consistent with the idea that God generally works in the world through the processes of nature. Yet there are serious limitations on attempts to project this idea into the most distant future. The future really does differ from the past. We have experience and memory of the past, and on that basis we come to some understanding of laws of nature. With those laws we attempt to predict the future, but we have no scientific observations of that future. As we try to peer further and further ahead in time, our predictions must become very general and lose contact with specific details of what might happen.

To see what this means, consider the state of the universe about half a million years after the big bang, the time at which we observe the microwave background radiation. Space is filled with radiation and a mixture of hydrogen and helium gases at a temperature of a few thousand degrees, continuing to expand and cool. The ways in which the amounts of radiation and matter would change from that point on could be calculated from the laws of physics. In principle, it could be determined from the situation at that epoch whether the cosmic expansion will eventually reverse or whether it will expand forever. But there is nothing to indicate that anything like *life* is going to develop. Something genuinely new is eventually going to come about, even though there is no sign of it at that point of cosmic history.

Paul is willing to speak about things which we know about in the world today when he responds to the question, "How are the dead raised? With what kind of body do they come?" (1 Corinthians 15:35). He goes on to remind his readers that there are different kinds of bodies of living things on earth, that there are heavenly bodies and earthly bodies, and that the seed that falls into the ground becomes a quite different body when it grows. But none of these examples is proof of the resurrection or a description of the way the resurrection of the dead will take place. They are analogies to help Christians to have some mental framework in which to think about the resurrection. Belief in the resurrection itself, and in the future in which "death has been swallowed up in victory" (1 Corinthians 15:54), is based on the resurrection of Jesus, the theme of the first half of 1 Corinthians 15.

We should think of anything which evolutionary biology or physical cosmology can contribute to this discussion in a similar way. These sciences may provide useful ideas or pictures, but our belief in God's future is not limited by them.

The Bible speaks of "new heavens and a new earth," not just the same old thing. God is faithful to creation, but God is going to do something surprising with it. The Bible uses the image of the thief in the night to bring out the unexpected character of God's act (Matthew 24:43). And in the climactic vision of the book of Revelation (21:5) God says, "See, I am making all things new."

The universe ultimately is in the hands of the one who has created and sustained and saved and hallowed it. The reminder given in the letter of James (4:13-16) for daily life is also relevant here:

> *Come now, you who say, "Today or tomorrow we will go to such and such a town and spend a year there, doing business and making money." Yet you do not even know what tomorrow will bring. What is your life? For you are a mist that appears for a little while and then vanishes. Instead you ought to say, "If the Lord wishes, we will live and do this or that." As it is, you boast in your arrogance; all such boasting is evil.*

Some humility is appropriate as we try to use even our best science to learn about, and to exert some control over, the future.

Topics For Discussion

1. What do we mean when we pray "Thy kingdom come" in the Lord's Prayer? What are we supposed to mean?

2. Why is the idea of resurrection of the body important?

3. Time travel is an important plot device in science fiction but has also been discussed seriously by some physicists. Are there any ways in which this concept could help us to understand the relationship between the resurrection of Jesus and God's final future?

1. This image is used in other places in the New Testament, such as Revelation 1:7. It goes back to the vision described in Daniel 7:13-14.

2. Wolfhart Pannenberg, *Jesus — God and Man*, 2nd ed. (Westminster, Philadelphia, 1977), p. 67.

Chapter 15

The Church's Mission

What is the church's mission in a scientific and technological world? In a fundamental way it is the same mission which the church has always had, to "make disciples of all nations" (Matthew 28:19). But those who work to make disciples need to know something of the culture and thought patterns of those to whom they address the gospel. Just as the church had to take account of Greek philosophy and Roman political structures when it moved from Palestine into the larger Mediterranean world, today it must take science and technology into account in order for its message to gain a hearing.

Those who have read this far have presumably had some interest in the issues which science and technology raise for Christianity and the questions which Christian theology may ask of scientists, and may simply have enjoyed the challenge of thinking about the Christian faith in some new ways. Some readers may have felt that certain scientific concepts which have been presented here are challenges to basic aspects of the Christian faith, and that Christianity needs to be defended from them. Others may think that the church is behind the times in adjusting to scientific discoveries. But regardless of how we see individual discoveries and theories, the world in which the church lives, and in which it must carry out its mission, is a world which is increasingly scientific and technological. The final questions we should ask have to do with ways in which the church can carry out its mission both *in* this world and *to* it. What areas of ministry (both of clergy and laypeople) need to take the developments which we've discussed into account?

The answer, briefly, is "Almost all of them!" There is very little of the church's work which cannot benefit from engagement with science. The point was put very clearly by the editor of a collection of papers from a conference which dealt with this topic: "Today's churches have no other place to fulfill their mission than a world whose basic assumptions are pervaded more and more by science."[1]

This doesn't mean that scientific ideas and new technologies always have to be in the forefront of the church's work. A great deal of the time they shouldn't be. But Christians who are aware of these realities can sometimes avoid mistakes and look for connections with the experience of people in ways which may be helpful for winning and keeping disciples.

The most obvious way in which scientific ideas come into play here is probably in the church's doing of theology — that is, its thinking about its beliefs — and in its teaching of the Christian faith. That is the activity in which we have been involved throughout most of this book. We have been trying to see how scientific discoveries can be understood within the Christian view of the world, and how they may require us to rethink some traditional ways of expressing Christian teachings.

This sort of activity needs to take place at all levels of the church. Academic theologians and seminary education should be involved in some study at the science-theology interface. That study, like all that is done in theological education, should not be seen as simply scholarly work for its own sake. It is done to prepare men and women for the ministry of the church, to carry out some of the further tasks which we're going to outline here. Pastors don't need to be experts in scientific disciplines, but they also should not be afraid to have them discussed. There is a big difference between saying, "I don't know but I'll look at it," and "Let's not get into that."

Science and technology should also be taken into account in sensitive ways in the educational programs of parishes. Young children will learn about creation from the first chapters of Genesis, and these can simply be presented to them as stories of God making the world, without any scientific issues being raised. But when children ask how the dinosaurs (or "ape men," or whatever) fit in, something needs to be said *at an appropriate level* which respects both science and Scripture. As children become older, they are of course able to think about these matters in more sophisticated ways and will have more exposure to them in their educational experience outside the church. The approach which we have taken in this book to the topic of divine action in the world begins with God's providential activity today and then moves to creation in the beginning. That emphasis on God as the one who creates and sustains the life of each person provides a good way to introduce the doctrine of creation both for young people and for adults, though understanding of creation also needs to be broadened beyond that to include questions about origins and the environment.

In addition to general discussions of science and religion, some of the specific topics which have been discussed in earlier chapters need to be dealt with in the educational programs of congregations. For example, many people today find themselves in situations in which they have to make decisions about questions of biomedical ethics. They may, on rather short notice, need to decide about what measures of life support are appropriate for an elderly relative or whether or not organs of an accident victim should be donated. Some understanding of theological and ethical principles should go into such decisions, and education about those principles can't wait until the time when decisions have to be made in the emergency room or the intensive care waiting area. It is important that some informed discussion about these issues take place in a relatively unstressful learning environment, so that people will have some background for decisions when the time comes to make them.

Preaching, the proclamation of the gospel, is a central feature of the church's ministry. What is to be proclaimed is Christ and the forgiveness of sins and acceptance of the sinner for his sake. Lectures on scientific discoveries or the dangers of technology, no matter how competent they are, are not sermons. But on the other hand, the gospel is proclaimed to people living in a scientific world. The things which threaten them and the hopes that they have often are connected with scientific or technological developments. Watching a program on cosmology on public television may fill people with a sense of the vastness and antiquity of the universe and make them wonder whether a cozy view of the world which they were taught in Sunday School can be of any relevance in such a universe. A sermon on Psalm 8 or Ephesians 1, texts which place God's concern for humanity in a truly cosmic setting, could make use of some of our reflection on anthropic principles of Chapter 9 in order to bring out the continuing relevance of the biblical message.

People who are afraid that evolutionary teaching must be destructive of belief in creation can be helped by the right kind of sermon on either of the two Genesis creation accounts.

The preacher will not naively view science and technology as good in all their expressions. The Christian message is not simply to be adapted to whatever current intellectual fashions happen to be. There are dangers, not because knowledge or power are bad in themselves, but because human beings can use them in the wrong ways and place too much confidence in them. Scientific understanding and technological power can be made into idols. Chapter 10 notes several biblical texts which speak to the proper use of technology and the dangers of its misuse.

Occasionally an entire sermon might address some of these concerns. Perhaps more frequent would be the modest use of some scientific concepts simply as illustrations in the course of a sermon. When Jesus says, "And I, when I am lifted up from the earth, will draw all people to myself" (John 12:32), the image which naturally comes to mind today is that of a magnet. Almost everyone has refrigerator magnets, and people don't have to have any special expertise in electromagnetic theory or engineering to understand what they do. The picture of a magnet drawing pieces of iron to itself can bring out vividly one way of thinking about the effect of the cross.

The sacraments of Baptism and the Lord's Supper make some contact with science and technology because of their fundamentally material character. Water and bread and wine are the same types of things which science studies. A great deal of sensitivity should be exercised with liturgical language, and scientific jargon should not intrude on the sacraments in clumsy ways. But education about the sacraments can bring out some important connections. Awareness of the remarkable physical properties of water which make it one of the essentials for life may heighten the awareness of what baptism means. The fact that in the Lord's Supper we use not bare grain and grapes but those things processed by human technology says something about the value which God confers upon technology as well as upon the material world itself.

Secondary features of worship such as hymns and other music may be considered here too. Hymns don't need to be filled with modern scientific language, but they also shouldn't reflect the earth-centered world view of the Middle Ages. More good hymns which take some account of the ways in which we see the universe today are needed.

Services of healing provide opportunities for reflection on the types of things we considered in Chapter 11. The anointing of the sick, whether for individuals or in a corporate service, should be seen first of all as symbolic prayer for God's healing through medical means. There are also a number of environmental observances — Rogationtide, Stewardship of Creation Sunday, Earth Sunday, and others — which various churches observe. And commemorations of Christians who have worked in science, engineering, and medicine can help to remind people of the appropriateness of these areas of work as vocations for Christians. The calendar of the *Lutheran Book of Worship*, for example, includes commemorations of the scientists Nicolaus Copernicus and Leonhard Euler and the nurses Florence Nightingale and Clara Maass; and the *Book of Common Prayer* commemorates Robert Grosseteste, an English bishop who was one of the important scientific thinkers of the Middle Ages. These considerations point out not only possibilities for worship services, but also ways in which science and technology should be involved in certain types of social action, such as care for the environment and health concerns.

Another type of social action in which churches might be engaged is encouragement of good science education, both for those seeking to go into scientific, engineering, and medical professions and for the general public. Scientific illiteracy is a serious danger for any society in today's world; it also is a danger for the church in some distinctive ways. Ignorance of science leaves Christians open to scare tactics of some groups who want to oppose certain scientific developments on religious grounds. Scientific illiteracy also creates a fertile field for cults such as the "Church of Scientology" which make use of pseudoscience.

The role of religious views in connection with teaching of evolution in public schools has been a hotly debated topic in the United

States. By law, teachers cannot present a particular religious view as the true faith and cannot try to convert students. But they can teach *about* religious views which are important in society, and churches should be concerned to see that such teaching about Christian understandings of creation is accurate and is not dominated either by the idea that Genesis is simply myth or that it must be read as historical narrative. Attempts to force public schools to present creation as a *scientific alternative* to evolution gives students the message that they must make a choice between "creation or evolution." If they were carried out, such programs are likely to push some students to abandon Christianity if they think that the evidence for evolution is strong! Christians should therefore resist such attempts, even if they themselves are generally skeptical about evolution.

Scientific and technological literacy should also be encouraged by Christian mission work in developing countries. It is an important component of liberation for people in limited economic circumstances. Without science and technology, they will never be able to compete in an industrialized world.

These final few pages have merely sketched some ways in which the mission of the church might be involved with scientific and technological issues in profitable ways. Each Christian, and each congregation, will be able to come up with other ways in which the things we have discussed here can contribute to its mission.

Topics For Discussion

1. What are some ways in which your congregation could be involved with issues of science, technology, and medicine?

2. Do any of the hymns which your congregation sings make use of modern scientific pictures of the world? Do any of them use outdated images or language?

3. Which religious views of creation should be presented in public schools?

---

1. John M. Mangum (editor), *The New Faith-Science Debate* (Fortress, Minneapolis, 1989), p. vi.

For Further Reading

Barbour, Ian G., *Science and Religion: Historical and Contemporary Issues.* (HarperCollins, New York, 1997). A thorough treatment by one of the major figures in the modern science-theology dialogue.

Cole-Turner, Ronald, *The New Genesis: Theology and the Genetic Revolution.* (Westminster/John Knox, Louisville, Kentucky, 1993). New developments in genetics and a theological interpretation of them.

Edwards, Denis, *The God of Evolution* (Paulist, New York, 1999). A trinitarian theology of evolution.

Einstein, Albert, and Infeld, Leopold, *The Evolution of Physics: From early concepts to relativity and quanta.* (Simon and Schuster, New York, New York, 1938). A description for laypeople by the greatest physicist of the twentieth century and one of his co-workers.

Hearn, Walter R., *Being a Christian in Science* (InterVarsity, Downers Grove, Illinois, 1997). A guide to the opportunities and challenges of scientific work as a vocation for Christians.

Jaki, Stanley L, *Science and Creation* (Scottish Academic, Edinburgh, 1986). A discussion of the relationship between the biblical view of the world and the development of science by a Roman Catholic theologian, physicist, and historian of science.

Hefner, Philip, *The Human Factor: Evolution, Culture, and Religion.* (Fortress, Minneapolis, Minnesota, 1993). An attempt to understand humanity theologically as a species created by God through evolutionary processes.

Lindberg, David C. and Numbers, Ronald L. (editors), *God and Nature: Historical Essays on the Encounter between Christianity and Science* (University of California, Berkeley, California, 1986). Essays by a number of scholars on different aspects of the relationship between science and Christianity from the time of the early church through the twentieth century.

Mangum, John M. (editor), *The New Faith-Science Debate: Probing Cosmology, Technology, and Theology* (Fortress, Minneapolis, Minnesota, 1989). A good introductory collection of essays from a global consultation on science and technology and the church, held in Cyprus in 1987.

Murphy, George L., Althouse, LaVonne, and Willis, Russell, *Cosmic Witness: Commentaries on Science/Technology Themes.* (CSS, Lima, Ohio, 1996). Discussions of biblical texts which are relevant to issues of science, technology, and medicine.

Murphy, Nancey, *Reconciling Science and Theology: A Radical Reformation Perspective* (Pandora, Kitchener, Ontario, 1997). An introductory overview of science-theology relationships from the Anabaptist tradition.

Peters, Ted, *Playing God?* (Routledge, New York, 1997). A theological discussion of "genetic determinism and human freedom."

Polkinghorne, John, *The Faith of a Physicist* (Princeton University, Princeton, New Jersey, 1994). A systematic discussion following the organization of topics in the Nicene Creed.

Santmire, H. Paul, *The Travail of Nature: The Ambiguous Ecological Promise of Christian Theology.* (Fortress, Philadelphia, 1985). A study of Christian attitudes toward nature from the Bible through the mid-twentieth century.

Smith, John Maynard, *The Problems of Biology.* (Oxford, New York, New York, 1986). A brief presentation of several important areas of biological research, including heredity, evolution, and the origin of life.

Teilhard de Chardin, Pierre, *Hymn of the Universe.* (Harper & Row, New York, 1965). The spirituality of the priest and paleontologist whose ideas have been quite influential on Christian thinking about evolution.

Torrance, Thomas F., *Preaching Christ Today: The Gospel and Scientific Thinking.* (William B. Eerdmans, Grand Rapids, Michigan, 1994). Two addresses dealing with relationships between theological and scientific methods and the proclamation of the gospel.